LORING THE

INBURGH

TO

GLASGOW

CANALS

(THE UNION CANAL, THE FORTH & CLYDE CANAL)

Hamish Brown

British Waterways
Edinburgh : The Stationery Office

©The Stationery Office limited 1997

First published 1997

Applications for reproduction should be made to
The Stationery Office Limited, South Gyle Crescent,
Edinburgh EH19 9EB

Acknowledgements:

The Stationery Office acknowledges with thanks the financial
assistance given by British Waterways in the preparation of this
book. Thanks are also due to the contributors of the illustrations:
British Waterways (Jill Richards) x, 88, (Helen Rowbotham) xiv,
xiv, 7, 24, 29, Edinburgh City Library: title page, 4, Dr. Patricia
Macdonald: vi, 94, Linlithgow Union Canal Society (Dr. Judy
Gray) 16, 18, Mr. Guthrie Hutton 21, 87, William Patrick
Library, Kirkintilloch (East Dumbarton Council) 49, 60. All
other photographs by Hamish Brown, Scottish Photographic.
The author would like to add his thanks to all of the above plus
the following; Sheila Galliomore, The Linlithgow Union Canal
Society (Mel and Judy Gray), Ronnie Rusack of the Canal
Centre and Bridge Inn, Ratho.

British Library Cataloguing in Publication Data.

A catalogue record of this book is available from the British
Library

All facts have been checked as far as possible but the author and
publishers cannot be held responsible for any errors, however
caused.
The author and publishers will welcome information on
changes or other helpful comments.

Cover photograph: Cruise and restaurant barges moored at
Glasgow Bridge.
Title page photograph: A winter scene at one of the Edinburgh
canal basins in olden days. (© Edinburgh City Library)

ISBN 0 11 495735 5

CONTENTS

Kilometres 0   1   2
Miles 0   1

N

STIRLING

CAMPSIE FELLS

Carron Valley
Resr

Pages 54 & 55

Pages
36 & 37

3

A81

A809

KILPATRICK HILLS

Pages 66 & 67

KILSYTH

Pages 76 & 77

6

MILNGAVIE

5

River Kelvin

KIRKINTILLOCH

CUMBERNAULD

River Avon

RIVER CLYDE

A80

M73

Hillend
Resr

A89

M8

GLASGOW

PAISLEY

AIRDRIE

M8

A726

A749

River Clyde

MOTHERWELL

A73

HAMILTON

EAST
KILBRIDE

A723

M74

A72

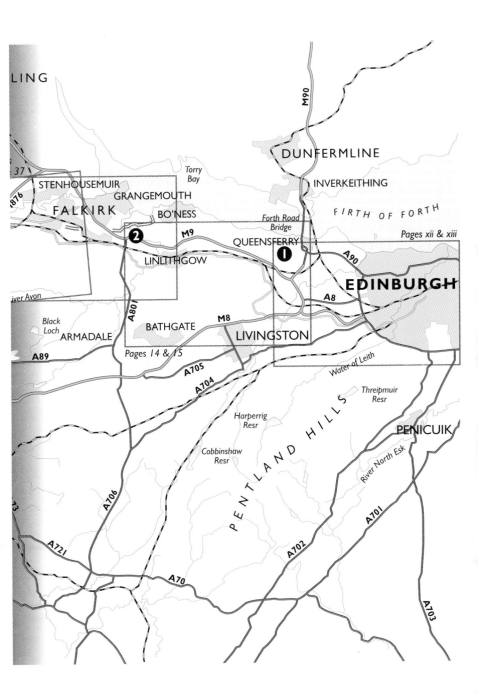

STIRLING

STENHOUSEMUIR

GRANGEMOUTH

BO'NESS

FALKIRK

Torry
Bay

M9

LINLITHGOW

River Avon

Black
Loch

ARMADALE

BATHGATE

M8

A801

A89

Pages 14 & 15

A705

A704

A706

A721

A70

DUNFERMLINE

INVERKEITHING

M90

FIRTH OF FORTH

Forth Road
Bridge

QUEENSFERRY

Pages xii & xiii

A90

A8

EDINBURGH

LIVINGSTON

Water of Leith

Threipmuir
Resr

Harperrig
Resr

PENICUIK

Cobbinshaw
Resr

River North Esk

P E N T L A N D   H I L L S

A702

A701

A703

1

2

INTRODUCTION

The towpaths of the Union and Forth & Clyde canals offer some of the pleasantest and quietest walking in the country and, with the historic towns on the route and the major fascination of the Antonine Wall, can give the visitor plenty to explore over many visits.

This book describes the canals from east to west in logical progression and there would be as much to be gained in treating it as a long-distance footpath guide, as in using it for making smaller day walks. Situated as the canals are in the centre of Scotland, they can give equally pleasant walking on a sunny summer evening or a winter day when hills and Highlands might be inadvisable. Good stretches are accessible to wheelchair users.

The major recommended access points are Central Edinburgh, Wester Hailes (Calder Quay), Ratho, Broxburn, Winchburgh, Linlithgow, Falkirk (Glen Bridge, Greenbank, Union Inn), Bonnybridge, Kilsyth, Kirkintilloch, Glasgow Bridge, Cadder, Bishopbriggs and any of the bridges in Glasgow. These all have some public transport to or from the cities and no parking problems for motorists. All these places would allow wheelchair access.

Recognised access points have the capital **A** surrounded by a sandy coloured box in the margin, and where wheelchairs could be used the **A** surrounded by a green coloured box (an * alongside the green box warns of excessive steepness or kerbs). The linear nature of the canals allows you to be dropped off at one place and picked up at another over almost any distance, or you can use public transport and walk the whole way bit by bit. Best of all, perhaps, would be to take a week and walk end-to-end to enjoy that special freedom and all the interests on the way.

A

A *

As all road, footpath and other signs along the route show distances in miles, they are given that way in this book. Heights from the map are perforce given in metres, an unavoidable inconsistency

Opposite: Slateford Aqueduct from the air. (© Dr Patricia Macdonald)

due to our botched ideas of going metric. Historical statistics are given in both imperial and metric measure.

Each chapter heading is followed by the numbers of the Ordnance Survey (OS) maps covering that section. OSLR means Ordnance Survey Landranger, scale 1:50,000, and OSPF means Ordnance Survey Pathfinder, scale 1:25,000. The Landrangers cover the canals on sheets 66, 65, 64. The more detailed Pathfinder numbers are 407, 406, 419, 405, 393, 404, 416, 403, and these will probably be found the most useful.

The canal is steadily being improved, and hedge-trimming, engineering works and the like can cause temporary closure to sections. Despite being a man-made structure it has a substantial wildlife population of great interest: trees, marsh and water plants and aquatic life as well as the more visual birdlife. (It is quite a thought on a busy Glasgow street that ducks may be paddling overhead!)

Dogs should be kept under control in order not to cause disturbance - or endanger other users, especially cyclists. The canal towpath is a great place to exercise dogs and there are generally no restrictions. Don't allow dogs to foul the towpath. A plea to cyclists, with whom the towpaths are rightly popular - always give warning of your approach, and please be prepared to give way to walkers. Too few of you do either at present!

Much about canals in general and specific features in particular appears in the main text, but a few comments may be of interest here. Canals are becoming 'popular recreational resources' which I presume means they are 'fun places' - and so they are. But how many people know much about canals?

In their heyday, the lack of locks on the Union Canal allowed travellers a speedy crossing between the cities of Edinburgh and Glasgow. The once-thriving service took as little as 13 hours, and cost the equivalent of 7½ pence. At one time there were plans to run the canal through Princes Street Gardens in Edinburgh and down to Leith Docks, but fierce opposition blocked this extension.

The concept and planning of the canals was marked throughout by dissention. The Forth & Clyde Canal opened in 1790, the Union Canal in 1822, but with an inter-city railway opening as early as the 1840s, they then began a century of decline. Now, for recreational purposes, both canals are slowly being brought back to life. Covered in a scum of weed, decades of litter, and overgrown, they are still a precious asset, and I hope all of us who walk their lengths will become champions in their defence and restoration. At the end there is a list of bodies who are actively engaged in using and/or restoring the canals. They are always glad to welcome new members.

Look out for details of construction. Bridges on the Union Canal are numbered from Edinburgh and there are 62 of them, plus several new ones and, of course, all those where the canal does the bridging, which is often much more exciting. Tow ropes have often worn grooves into stonework, there are mile posts, wharves, winding-holes for turning boats and odd features on the bridges.

The new 31½-mile Union Canal was nicknamed The Mathematical River, partly because it followed the 240-ft (73m) contour, and also because it maintained a regular width (35 ft/11m) and depth (5 ft/1.5m). While on figures, in 1834 no fewer than 121,407 passengers travelled the canal. Meals, music, even gaming tables were provided to pass the time, and there was a night sleeper service which was popular with both businessmen and honeymoon couples.

Linlithgow Palace was garrisoned as the local people were doubtful about the wild Irish navvies on their doorstep. Two have gained deserved notoriety through a second career as body-snatchers - their names being Burke and Hare. Ironically, much of the expertise gained on building the canals was then used in the construction of the railways that led to the death of the canals.

The 35 mile Forth & Clyde Canal was a much bigger undertaking as it was to carry sea-going craft (avoiding the dangers of sailing north about Scotland). Its width was set at 28ft (8m) and it was 8ft (2.7m) deep. It was officially 'closed' in 1963 and many roads were unfortunately allowed to culvert sections of the canal.

The Forth & Clyde Canal started at Grangemouth in 1768 (it was only opened in 1790 as funds ran out during construction) and this is often claimed to be the first canal cutting in Scotland, a fact which, as a Fifer, I cannot let pass unchallenged. The first canal known in Scotland was at Upper Largo, when the great naval hero Sir Andrew Wood (c.1455-1539) had some of his captive English crews dig a canal from Largo House to the local kirk so he could be rowed to church in his admiral's barge. This was at the end of the 15th century.

The first proposal for a canal to link the Forth and the Clyde came from Charles II. He was very much into naval and engineering progress but, alas, was usually into debt as well. It's an interesting speculation that had he not poured money into the mole at Tangier, there might just have been monies for a canal across Scotland.

It is hard to envisage the Scotland of pre-canal times, when the only transport was four-footed, either as riding and pack animals or pulling inefficient carts over an almost impossible landscape. With Glasgow and Edinburgh growing and both domestic and industrial demand for coal reaching a critical stage, there had to be some new development. The Forth & Clyde Canal was a splendid pioneering venture and, not for the first time, Edinburgh took years of squabbling over routes and plans before it followed with the Union Canal. (I notice that the Edinburgh provost, who bitterly opposed the finally accepted plan of Thomas Baird, has his name down among the subscribers.) John Rennie's plans were thus superseded. Thomas Telford had supported Baird, who consulted him on various occasions

It is also hard to envisage the sheer scale of the work. The whole length was divided into lots and these were allocated to various contractors. It was all pick, shovel and wheelbarrow work, employing thousands of itinerant labourers. The squalor can be imagined. A satellite picture of the time would have shown a dirty brown scar across Scotland. The scar would hardly have healed before the railways were making the canals redundant.

Despite the long set-back the canals can still be walked, almost in their entirety; safe, scenic walking with many places of interest along the way still to be enjoyed. You can be as energetic or lazy as you wish, enjoying the variations of the seasons and the good company of friends as you explore, from city to city, the heart of Scotland.

A horse-drawn barge in the canal's heyday.

Swan and cygnets, a common sight on the canals.

Walking a quiet stretch on the Union Canal.

See pages 14 and 15 for next map

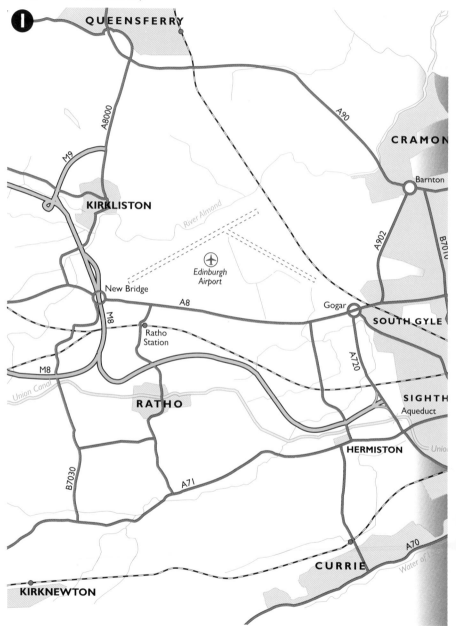

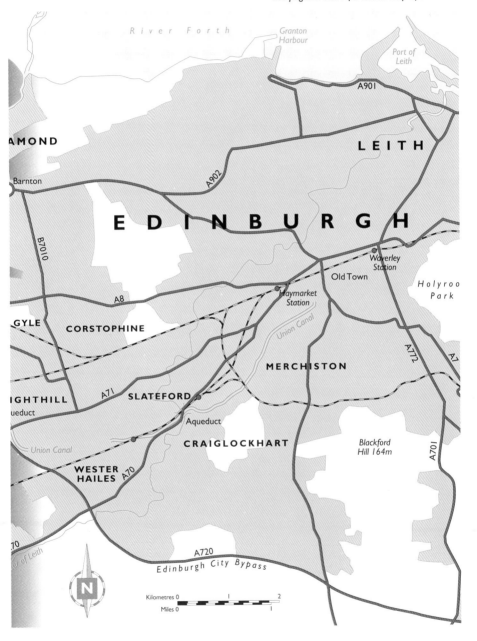

See pages iv and v for overall map of the canals

River Forth

Granton
Harbour

Port of
Leith

A901

AMOND

LEITH

Barnton

A902

EDINBURGH

B7010

Waverley
Station

Old Town

Holyroo
Park

A8

Haymarket
Station

GYLE

CORSTOPHINE

Union Canal

A772

A7

MERCHISTON

A71

IGHTHILL

SLATEFORD

ueduct

Aqueduct

Union Canal

CRAIGLOCKHART

Blackford
Hill 164m

A701

WESTER
HAILES

A70

70

r of Leith

A720

Edinburgh City Bypass

N

Kilometres 0   1   2
Miles 0   1

An Edinburgh Canal Society Water Festival at Harrison Park in 1991. (© British Waterways)

Rafts at a Wester Hailes Gala some years ago. (© British Waterways)

CHAPTER ONE

EDINBURGH

TO THE

ALMOND AQUEDUCT

OSLR 66, OSPF 407, 406, 419

The Edinburgh start to exploring the canals gives a strange feeling, for instead of the bustling basins crowded with boats and sails, horses and people, there is silence and emptiness. Without help it would be very difficult even to find the Edinburgh end of the canals so this is done from two convenient places, the west end of Princes Street and Haymarket Station.

From the west end of Princes Street head south along Lothian Road, passing the Usher Hall (off left) and the Sheraton Hotel and Edinburgh Filmhouse (right) to reach Morrison Street. The cinema building (Lothian House, 1922) on the corner of Morrison Street stands on the original Hopetoun Basin, named after the Earl of Hopetoun, whose collieries supplied much of Edinburgh's coal. High on the Lothian Road face of this fine building is a mural showing a barge being towed, best seen from across the busy road.

Walk on past the cinema, still on Lothian Road, and turn right at the next junction onto Fountainhall. Fat Sam's is in the original Meat Market and is dated 1884. The Co-operative Society Building stands by what was Port Hamilton, named after the Duke of Hamilton. The Port Hamilton Tavern across the street is another pointer to this past connection. The present east end of the canal lies behind the sheds and yards behind the pub. Lochrin Basin, built for the Haig Whisky works, lies further over but has also vanished under subsequent developments. Continue along Fountainbridge.

From Haymarket Station, head up Morrison Street as far as the new International Conference Centre and turn right along Gardiner's Crescent (the West Approach Road passes underneath) to reach Fountainbridge. The Port Hamilton Tavern will be noticed diagonally left across the junction. Turn right along Fountainbridge, which is dominated by the Scottish & Newcastle Fountain Brewery site. The wall on the left has some sculpted murals and the house on the corner of Grove Street is an architectural survival, an ornate 1864 tenement.

Further along, there is the obvious Fountain Brewery clock over the pavement. Turn left into Gilmore Park and soon reach the canal with its interesting lifting bridge. This originally stood on Fountainbridge near the Port Hamilton Tavern and is inscribed Leamington Bridge. By walking left, the present end of the canal can soon be reached; nearby lay the Lochrin Basin. This rump of water is used by canoeists and slalom poles hang over the water. It was once the scene of a headline-grabbing accident.

Canoeists on the canal at Fountainbridge.

George Meikle Kemp was the creator of the Scott Monument, a shy, rather odd character whose design was only chosen because of an impasse in awarding the contract to the first choices. He was the compromise candidate. More joiner than architect, his design incorporated ideas ranging from Melrose Abbey to Rouen Cathedral, but then, Scott himself was constantly stealing ideas if not actual structures as he built Abbotsford, his house near Melrose.

Kemp had been to see his contractor (the stone presumably coming on the Union Canal) and left to walk home along the towpath on a cold, dark, foggy night. Somehow he lost his bearings and walked off the pier near the Lochrin Distillery. A week later the first evidence of a tragedy appeared when his stick and hat floated to the surface. He is buried in St Cuthbert's, the church down in the dell below the meeting of Princes Street and Lothian Road. Others buried there include Alexander Nasmyth (whose bridge you will see on the Almond) and the drug-addict writer Thomas de Quincy.

Head out on the north bank from the lifting bridge; throughout its length the towpath is on this side of the Union Canal. The first mile or so is a bit seedy with factories and works, odd touches of murals and the ubiquitous swans, ducks, coots and moorhens, which are not at all perturbed at humans passing so near. One pair of swans nest here.

The next bridge, Viewforth, has a carved castle over its keystone on the east, and a tree with fish, on the west: symbols of Edinburgh and Glasgow, the original full name of the canal being the Glasgow and Edinburgh Union Canal.

There are new flats across the canal, then Yeaman Place bridge (no access) leads to a long sweep with older tenements on either side. The canal bears left and Polwarth Parish Church lies ahead with the Harrison Park and bowling green on the right. Harrison Road crosses the canal by an iron bridge and there's the first of several boathouses across on the south side. At the end of the park (Ogilvie Terrace) there is a launching slip, British Waterways notice board, a string of boats, the Edinburgh Canal Centre boathouse and a winding hole. The big iron bridge, with spiky finials, carries Ashley Terrace and is inscribed 'Lockhart Bridge 1904'. Continuing, the houses stand back from the banks and the feeling is more rural.

A rather weathered milestone is the next landmark, just before the boathouses on the far bank, and then the canal bestrides a railway line which is backed by a view of Corstorphine Hill with its masts (and Edinburgh Zoo). There is also a canal overflow on this bank.

The next bridge turns out to be two bridges and, just before them, right, is the Edinburgh University Rowing Club boatshed. The first (North Meggetland) bridge is a modern concrete structure, the second (Meggetland) is the first surviving example of the original Union Canal bridges, the style of which will become very familiar as we progress; it bears the number 4, the bridges being numbered from the Edinburgh end. Meggetland is the home of Boroughmuir RFC and there are extensive Council playing fields, tennis courts, and a boathouse to the right as you continue. Another milestone has barely discernible numbers on it, then there is a series of pipes in conjunction with a footbridge crossing from Allan Park Road on the north to Craiglockhart on the south.

The canal wiggles along its contour to reach the next landmark, the Prince Charlie Aqueduct, which was rebuilt in 1937, one of the better concrete bridges of that vintage when seen from the Slateford Road, which it spans. The name perhaps comes from the Pretender setting up camp in the vicinity in 1745 to await the surrender of the city. A flight of steps leads down and a nearby newsagent's shop offers basic refreshments.

Beyond, industrial works lie below to the right while the Pentlands loom on the left front, but then comes the most spectacular structure within the city, the eight-arched Slateford

Slateford Aqueduct in early days. (© Edinburgh City Library)

Aqueduct, 152m (500 ft) long and 23m (75 ft) above the Water of Leith, with the waterway carried in an iron trough. It is now rather hemmed in by the busy Slateford Road to the south and a lower, but fine, arched railway bridge to the north. There is no access to allow an alternative viewpoint.

Another worn milestone stands at the west end of the aqueduct and the canal continues winding along to Redhall Park, where there is a footbridge and an underpass. To see the latter, turn off at the footbridge then bear left (right goes under the railway by a tunnel) along a path to the underpass, which is lined with setts and only offers about six feet of headroom. A path leads back onto the towpath. A railway bridges the canal then you come to the culverted blockage of Kingsknowe Road. Kingsknowe railway station lies immediately left, with trains into the city roughly every hour. Somewhere along the way you may have seen an old barge, afloat or sunken, which is thought to have carried ammunition into the city and is known as 'the gunboat'. It is periodically used when repairs are required to the city end of the canal.

Hailes Park has lost some of its area to flats, and here you reach the practical end of the city part of the Union Canal. There is a launching slip, winding basin and so on, at the west end of the park - and the canal just disappears. Immediately left, off

Dumbryden Road, is a supermarket. Hailes Park was once a quarry (30m/100 ft deep), much of the stone being sent to London. Dalry School, 1876, is built of Hailes stone.

The water of the canal is culverted for over a mile through Wester Hailes, so careful urban navigation is required to regain the canal when it re-emerges. Steps lead up onto a road; turn left to cross at once to a footpath marked by two bollards. This passes below the end of one of three huge metal-sheathed tower blocks and comes out to an area of grass and trees. Cross the access road of the tower blocks to follow a footpath and turn right at the second lamp post. Walk on, swinging up right past a pumping station and cut down to Hailesland Road at a bus stop.

Follow this big road under a pedestrian bridge and on to a roundabout. Beyond, bear left up Hailesland Place and turn right onto a paved pedestrian way outside the Hailesland Primary School/Children's Centre. This leads out to flats. Swing down, right, and then turn sharply left round the end of the last flat (Murrayburn Place sign) and on by a shrubbery to go through an underpass.

The pass leads back to the big road but then swings up left again to another mural-decorated underpass. (St John Ogilvie R.C. Church lies on the other side of the road, a building of no architectural merit.) The underpass leads to Wester Hailes Education Centre; turn right in front of this and follow the perimeter fence round and up. Continue along Calder Grove into Calder Crescent, go left, and on the left, there is an access point and quay for the canal, where you can start walking again (Calder Quay). For interest, first turn left and walk back to see the canal's re-appearance. You pass the Murray Burn flowing under the canal, a railed-off area indicating its presence. Where the canal starts (or ends) there's a turning basin. Water is pumped through this long break to keep the flow clean.

Return to Calder Quay and walk on to go under the abandoned A71 road bridge (Bridge 8) which is immediately preceded by the larger A71 concrete replacement. The canal then swings left (west) by the last three buildings of the Sighthill Industrial Estate, which sprawls away to the north-east, and comes to the 1987 Hermiston Aqueduct, now re-named the Scott Russell Aqueduct after the engineer and naval architect who pioneered the wave-line principle of ship construction following experiments on the canal in the 19th century.

The aqueduct soars 56m (170 feet) over the roaring traffic on the Edinburgh city bypass, an extraordinary place in a way, with the ultimate expression of the human rat-race below giving a crazy contrast with the rural calm of the view ahead through Bridges 9

View of the Edinburgh City Bypass from the canal aqueduct.

and 10. Bridge 9 is only used by a farm, and the road over Bridge 10 leads nowhere, being cut off by the M8 western approach motorway, opened in December 1995. Motorways and country calm are going to take turns for several miles to come. There's a basin for launching and turning by Bridge 10.

Next comes the novelty of a new bridge: Gogar Station Road Bridge, opened 1995, numbered 10A, and a praiseworthy attempt at a bit of style. Bridges come fast. Number 11 is grassy and abandoned and the short stretch to Bridge 12 looks across to the park-like grounds of Hermiston House, which has splendid big trees alongside the canal. There's a small basin west of Bridge 12, with an old barge in it, and the stretch westwards on to Ratho was, in 1995 anyway, the home of a pair of Australian black swans. There has been some tree planting on the banks here and there are some clear 'kicking stones', which you will see periodically all along the canal. These are stones set on the edge of the towpath to give the horses a safer purchase when straining to pull barges along. The next interest is a massive clean-lined aqueduct over the infant Gogar Burn.

The Jaw Bridge (13) soon follows. It only links farmland and like most of the minor bridges has iron railings rather than a stone parapet. Just past it is a milestone with 25/6 on it: 25 miles to Falkirk, 6 to Edinburgh. There's a spillway as you walk on towards the bigger Gogar Moor Bridge (14) which is a real hump-back at a blind junction, so is not a recommended access point. A 24/7 milestone lies in the small wood that follows but, on a bit, there's another 24/7 milestone so someone has booed! Ratho Park Golf Course across the canal has a very grand clubhouse and, off right, there are big open views back to Edinburgh Castle and Arthur's Seat.

The Honorable Society of Edinburgh Boaters on the Union Canal near Gogar. (© British Waterways)

Ratho appears ahead, the church, hall and manse standing out boldly on the right. New housing lies on the south side with several inflowing water channels, then you reach the first stage post, with a poor milestone by it. There's a big basin with a wharf on the south side (a longboat has been moored there for several years) and the traffic lights-controlled Bridge 15 crosses in front of the Bridge Inn.

In its heyday, Ratho had 14 pubs. The Pop Inn, next to the canal, is reputed to have had a door at each end of the building so the bargeman in charge of the towing horse could enter by one door, enjoy a pint *en passant,* and exit by the other door without having fallen behind his charge. About 1845 Ratho House was turned into a distillery, the annual production of 42,000 gallons being largely consumed locally. Canal work was obviously a drouthy business. Ratho was actually a change house and fare stage for tolls. A son of the Bridge Inn owners was the last person to be publicly hanged in Edinburgh, in May 1864.

One of Edinburgh's regular exports via the canal was manure (horses rather than horse power in those days) and this led to great fertility on the canalside farms. Maybe this lingers on, as two local farms hold world records for wheat production. Coal (and building stone) was the big import to the city, and the major reason for the canal being built. The passenger side was never lucrative and was killed by the railways.

The Bridge Inn was originally a farm, then a staging post on the canal, now it is renowned for the excellence of its food, the friendly service and delightful setting. The walls are covered with photographs of the canal in past days. It is also the base of the

Edinburgh Canal Centre, which offers both interpretation and activity. Boats can be hired and there is a variety of cruises on offer with the stately Ratho Princess, the small Almond Queen and the two famous restaurant longboats, the Pride of the Union and Pride of Belhaven. These often go along to the Almond Aqueduct where people dine on board ('in the air' it feels) or *al fresco* on the bank. There are even cruises to Santa's Secret Island in the festive season.

The Seagull Trust is also based here and runs free trips for disabled passengers in the Mackay Seagull and St John Crusader, (daily, Apr–Oct, tel: 0131-333-1320). Their first cruise took place here in 1979; now 5,000 people are involved annually and there are other boats based at Falkirk, Kirkintilloch, and Inverness.

A Ratho is a neat little village and, before continuing, do have a look

at the old cemetery round the church. Cross the bridge again (Baird Road commemorates one of the canal's engineers) and the church lies behind the war memorial. Left of the door is an unusual single stone shaped like a coffin; on its side the inscription indicates the incumbent suffered 'an instantaneous death' from a stroke by a threshing machine early last century.

The coffin-shaped gravestone in Ratho churchyard.

Ratho is a major access point and has car parks opposite the church and by the Bridge Inn. From the Newbridge roundabout turn off for Newbridge then, almost at once, off left and follow Edinburgh Canal Centre signs. Leaving Edinburgh by the A71, the turning off by Dalmahoy Road is similarly signposted.

Back on the canal, you pass the old change house and set off along a good towpath, away from the importuning ducks. Walk along the Ratho Hall grounds with some of Ratho's newer houses over to the south, then there is a peaceful woody section with mature trees shading both banks. Once out of the trees there is quite a contrast, for the M8 swings alongside the canal for a while to share its roar and bustle with you. There is a wider section, Wilkie's Basin, with an island in it, then you cross the B7030 road **A** * (Bonington Aqueduct) from Newbridge to Wilkieston, on an aqueduct which was reconstructed in 1978. Timbers dredged up in the basin are thought to be from one of the 'Swifts' which carried passengers from Edinburgh to Falkirk in three and a half hours. Pulled by two horses (changed periodically) they had prior right of way and charged along in style.

Having had quite a spell without bridges, numbers 16, 17 and 18 come in quick succession. By the attractive setting of Bridge 16 (Nellfield) you may see the longboat Thomas Telford moored. There is also a milestone and you are back in mature woods again, a gentle spot. Bridge 17 is a high arch with Clifton School to the north, Bridge 18 has a rustic feel (with fancy railings). Then, quite dramatically, you reach the high Almond Aqueduct. There is little warning: you round a bend and are on it. On the other side there is a basin, wharf and car park, and the major feeder for the canal flows in too. Upstream lies Almondell Country Park, which is well worth a diversionary visit and will be described separately.

The car park opposite can be reached from Newbridge, taking the B7030 which passes under railway, M8 and the Bonington Aqueduct. Follow 'Union Canal' signs thereafter. There is access to the aqueduct from the car park so even the disabled can see the spectacular setting. Long flights of steps however link the two sides of the canal. On the wall by the towpath is the date 1821. The drive passing under the canal is private, going to Lin's Mill. There is no mill now, but Lin's Grave is hidden away in the woods of the grounds and is inscribed 'Here lyeth the dust of William Lin richt heritor of Lins Miln who died in the year of the Lord 1645'. He was one of the many victims of the plague which ravished Scotland that year.

The boats cruising from Ratho often turn at this spot after sailing out and back 'over space' on the aqueduct. I've also seen them provide a buffet supper ashore and one wedding charter were thoroughly enjoying life. An 1834 handbill, offering ten-mile (16 km) trips for sixpence (2p) noted that here, "fruits, confectioneries and varieties of refreshment can be had". Now, sadly, litter louts just leave their chip supper debris behind.

Ratho's Bridge Inn is the base of many Union Canal activities.

CHAPTER TWO

ALMONDELL COUNTRY PARK

OSLR 65, OSPF 406, 419

This attractive park has canal associations, with the feeder canal flowing down it. The walk up from the canal is not suitable for wheelchairs, but the park can be reached by vehicle from East Calder, with plenty of wheelchair activity possible.

For Almondell Country Park, walk out from the canalside car park and after about 100m there are steps (signposted, right) which drop down to the feeder aqueduct, here going into a final tunnel to reach the canal basin. Turn left and walk up the glen. Across the way Illieston Castle stands boldly against the skyline, and downstream lies the canal aqueduct, a splendid, buttressed structure. Illieston Castle is a well-preserved tower house, built by John Ellis in 1665 but with earlier buildings going back much further. James II and James IV both used it as a hunting lodge.

There are some culverts and bridges as you contour the top of the fields. Quite a bit of restoration work was done in 1989 and 1990 as there were leaks and landslips affecting the feeder.

Cross a bridge (the river loops away from you here) and walk through pleasant beechwood. After passing under the line of pylons, drop down and along, picking up the feeder again for a quiet stretch to the entrance drive to Shiel Mill, where there is a stone bridge over the feeder. You then walk along a hawthorn hedge. The path is perfectly clear to follow, even if frequent stiles make it a bit of a steeplechase, and the feeder twice vanishes into conduits, these tunnels necessitated by the looping river pushing hard against the steep valley side, and leaving no room for a water channel and not much space for the path.

Where a flight of steps goes off left, a notice indicates the way you have come: 'Linns Mill Union Canal 1¾ miles'. You then cross a newish bridge of character, a graceful, single tower suspension bridge. A plaque is inscribed 'Mandela Bridge. Opened 1986 in tribute to those in South Africa who struggle for freedom and dignity. "The Cathedral of Peace is built of many small stones"'. Another plaque is a 1971 Civic Trust Award for the structural steel design of the bridge.

A grassy area, once the old walled garden of Almondell House, leads to the park's Visitor Centre buildings, in the stable block of the former mansion which had a connection with the antiquarian 11th Earl of Buchan. The Erskines were an interesting family. The 11th Earl was the last to live at nearby Kirkhill House, and much of its contents were taken to Almondell, which had been built by his brother Henry, whose son inherited the title in 1829.

Henry Erskine was a famous lawyer (he became Lord Advocate) and started building Almondell in 1790 to his own eccentric design. It was a disastrous enterprise, but he loved the setting which we enjoy today, with the additional benefit of the trees being in their splendid maturity. (The house was damaged by fire in the 1950s and demolished in 1969. Its site, which you pass later, is marked by a parking place for disabled drivers.)

On the road beyond the North Lodge of the park is an unobtrusive stone with an enigmatic dedication to William Wallace. Dated 1784, it doesn't take much guessing who erected it! The strangest structure the eccentric earl created was at Kirkhill, on the outskirts of Broxburn.

Mathematician, astronomer, antiquarian and scholar, the Earl of Buchan constructed a scale model of the Solar System in and around the grounds of Kirkhill House in 1776. The model consisted of the Sun, Mercury, Venus, the Earth and its moon, Mars, Jupiter and its four moons and Saturn with its rings and five moons. Mars is now known to have two moons, Jupiter eleven moons and Saturn nine, and since the construction of the model, Neptune, Uranus and Pluto have been discovered; but even bearing this in mind, the model was extraordinarily accurate. It was constructed to a scale of 12,238.28 miles to an inch (approximately 1:775 million), the Sun being represented by a stone sphere six feet in diameter, and the Earth by a bronze sphere 0.646 inches in diameter placed 645 feet (196m) away. The larger planets were made, like the Sun, of stone while the smaller planets were of bronze.

The model has disappeared, but a summary of the calculations which enabled the Earl to construct the model are preserved on the stone pillar which Buchan erected in the grounds of Kirkhill in 1777. The astronomical data inscribed on the pillar still largely holds true today. Buchan also included on the pillar a prediction of the position of the planets on 20 May 2255 (why he chose this date is unknown).

The pillar was surmounted by a bell tower, on top of which was a metal cross. After Buchan's death, the bell tower was removed and taken to his younger brother's estate at Almondell, where it was placed in front of the stables over a well (which is still there). The pillar remained at Kirkhill, but by the late 1970s it had collapsed. When the shell of Kirkhill House was sold for private restoration, the stones of the pillar were taken into safekeeping by West Lothian History and Amenity Society, and it was decided to rebuild the pillar, with bell tower and cross, in front of the Visitor Centre at Almondell.

The Visitor Centre is a lively, friendly place with interesting historical and wildlife displays, an aquarium and an audio-visual presentation. It is open during office hours from Monday to Thursday and on Sunday, but shut Friday and Saturday. Soft drinks, tea, snacks and chocolate are on sale if you need refreshments.

The astronomical pillar in the Almondell Country Park.

Continue up the main drive (there are some fine specimen trees including copper beech, cypress, sequoia and lime) to reach a ruined stone bridge designed by the portrait-painter Alexander Naismith (or Nasmythe or Naysmith) and built about 1800. (There are plans for its restoration, using money from the Heritage Lottery Fund. It is not unreasonable to say that as a bridge-builder, Naismith was a good painter.)

Continue upstream on the left bank path to reach a novel bridge, which is also the aqueduct of the canal feeder, an ingenious combination that allows pedestrians - almost - to walk on water. This unusual bridge dates from 1820, and is the work of Hugh Baird, engineer of the Union Canal. To keep the canal topped up, as much as two million gallons of water a day may be needed.

The next landmark is a lofty viaduct with a roofed structure like an exaggerated church porch below it (presumably in defence of people dropping things overboard) and it is worth climbing up to the roadway (a small bridge over the feeder leads to steep steps). This was once a railway viaduct (c. 1886) leading to Pumpherston, where oil shale was mined. The Calders and Pumpherston have now been overshadowed by Livingston New Town to the west. In 1962 Livingston's population was 2,000, now it is 37,000 with over 150 industries, and the huge Cameron Ironworks, the area's largest employer, making products for the offshore oil industry. The major oil processing plant at Grangemouth will be seen after Linlithgow. Considering the sprawl of industry, the canal walk retains a remarkably rural feel, right to the end.

Looking upstream, you can still see the feeder, but it is only a five-minute walk to the weir where the water is led off from the River Almond. Cobbinshaw Reservoir in the Pentland Hills was built to provide extra water, which flows down the Bog Burn and becomes the Muirieston Water, then joins the Linhouse Water in Mid Calder before finally running into the Almond. The River Almond, when it passes under the Union Canal, is 70 feet (22m) lower, hence the need to tap the river upstream.

The feeder channel here is full of monkey flower, bittersweet, greater willowherb (an aquatic cousin of the rose-bay species which is also plentiful) and blue water mint. Once you've wandered up to the weir, the diversion is over, and the route is retraced back to the Union Canal. Having seen all this engineering to gain water, it is odd that the aqueduct itself has a sluice for letting water out of the canal, but it is important in keeping water levels constant.

See pages 36 and 37 for next map

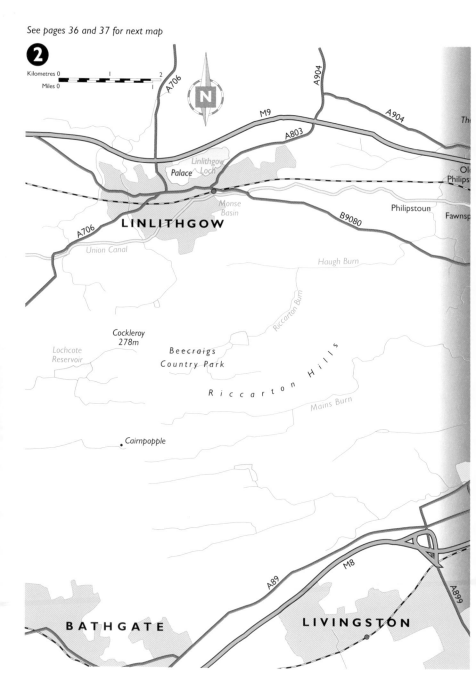

2

Kilometres 0 _____ 1 _____ 2
Miles 0 _____ 1

A706

N

A904

M9

A904

A803

The

Linlithgow
Loch
Palace

Ol
Philips

Monse
Basin

Philipstoun

Fawnsp

LINLITHGOW

A706

B9080

Union Canal

Haugh Burn

Riccarton Burn

Cockleroy
278m

Beecraigs
Country Park

Lochcote
Reservoir

Riccarton Hills

Riccarton Hills

Mains Burn

• Cairnpopple

M8

A89

A899

BATHGATE

LIVINGSTON

See pages xii and xiii for previous map

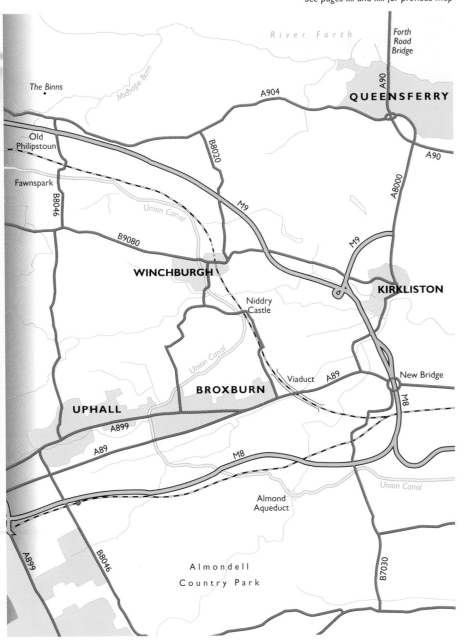

CHAPTER THREE

ALMOND AQUEDUCT

TO

WINCHBURGH

OSLR 65, OSPF 406

The aqueduct is impressively high and exposed with the narrow, cobbled pathway edged on the left by the iron trough of the canal. On the right, an airy iron railing does little to hide the 70 ft (22m) drop to the River Almond. There is a superb view north, down the river, to Telford's Almond Valley Viaduct on the main Edinburgh-Glasgow Railway. This was built in 1842 and, with 36 arches, it surpasses the canal's mere five.

The control sluice, in the middle of the south side, tends to dribble water and, in severe winters, this overflow has been known to freeze solid, creating a remarkable pillar of ice. At the west end of the aqueduct there is a milestone marked '10' (to Edinburgh) and '21' (to Falkirk). About 100m further on an overflow channel, lined with granite setts, crosses the towpath.

A bank prevents you from seeing any view, but the noise of the M8 will be noticed. The next bridge reached is numbered 19 on the arch, and just before it a minor road once gave access to a landing stage. Beyond Bridge 19 a hedge blocks the view for a while, then suddenly ends, and you are looking out onto an industrial landscape backed by shale bings and fronted by sweeping rail and motorway routes and, as like as not, aircraft at low altitude – Edinburgh Airport lies just beyond the great railway viaduct.

The canal, keeping to its contour line, does a big loop round Broxburn, but is cut by the M8, so you have to make a diversion. Leave the canal at Bridge 20, cross the bridge and walk on, round Muirend Farm, and continue past another farm charmingly

Opposite: The famous 1895 icicle on the Almond Aqueduct. (© LUCS)

17

named Lookabootye, which is also the motto of the county of Clackmannan. Drumshoreland House entrance is passed to reach a crossroads. Turn right ('Broxburn 1') and in turn snake under the railway and the M8 to regain the canal at Bridge 23. Passing under the railway gives blind bends and great care should be taken. As the canal is simply making a big loop round Broxburn (stuck on its contour) a safer option is to cut off at Bridge 20 and head north to reach the town. (This is described later.)

The railway is the old Edinburgh-Uphall-Bathgate-Coatbridge-Glasgow line, which breaks off from the main Edinburgh-Glasgow line west of Ratho (Newbridge Junction), and was originally built in 1849 to Bathgate, being extended to Airdrie and Glasgow in 1879. It served the coal, iron and shale oil industries, and the last passenger train was in 1956.

The creation of Livingston New Town failed to provide new passengers, and the line west to Airdrie was lifted in 1982. Bathgate station was gutted by an arsonist. Out of this dismal history came resurrection, and the line to Bathgate (an unusual

The Almond Aqueduct as it used to be. (© LUCS)

modern station) is now a busy commuter route. Redesigning the M8 to allow the canal to be used again is one of the major restoration tasks of the future. (You have skipped Bridges 21, lost between railway and M8, and 22 by Learielaw Farm). British Waterways have their Union Canal base beside Bridge 23, and the canal ranger's office is also here. If it is open, useful information can be obtained.

Continue on the towpath, noting the eye-shaped windows in the building up against the bridge. Pass milestone 19/11 and a small stream passing under the canal where the hedge has been properly 'layered'. Bridge 24 has what looks like Christmas decorations hanging overhead, to stop swans flying into the wires, and then, on the far side, there's a spillway into another burn.

The next bridge is an ugly red brick and iron structure for the modern A89, and Bridge 25 links a housing scheme with playing fields, with steps onto the towpath as you head north, cross the Brox Burn, and reach the A899, the main Uphall-Broxburn road (steps up), at a modern concrete bridge of no character. Turn right if you want Broxburn's town centre and, at the traffic lights in the centre, turn left again to rejoin the canal as it leaves the town.

Broxburn has a wide range of shops, coffee houses and pubs, and is a friendly place despite a rather unpretentious appearance. It straggles along north of the Brox Burn, and grew rapidly with the shale oil industry. In 1861 the population was 660, in 1891 it was 5,898. With that industry gone, there is a scruffy air of survival only. They were either affy wild or unco guid in Victorian times. I lost count of the churches

Bridge 23 and the British Waterways Union Canal H.Q.

along the long High Street that joins it with Uphall. The West Church is 'weird and wonderful Gothic', and the Roman Catholic church the real showpiece. St Nicholas Parish Church, on the B8046 out of Uphall, is the only old church. Uphall was once Strathbrock ('valley of badgers') and Broxburn is from the same old word brock for badger ('badger stream'). Uphall is a name which seems to cause pronunciation problems for some reason. It is just as written, Up-hall, but people will produce Uffle and such like.

The Earl of Buchan built his solar-system model at the family home, Kirkhill. The family were connected with the area until after the Second World War. Broxburn's Roman Catholic church was built in 1880 for the Dowager Countess of Buchan. She presented it with the font ,which has had a varied history. Dating to pre-Reformation times, it was ejected from the new kirk and for some time was used as a cattle water trough on a local farm. When it was recognised for what it was, the farmer gave it to the countess.

19

At the west end of Uphall is Houston House, a beautiful castle-mansion, once owned by Mary Queen of Scots' advocate, Sir John Shairp. The Shairp family lived there for 350 years: cavaliers and squires, lawyers, MPs, academics (Principal Shairp of The Bush Aboon Traquair, was a great walker and a minor poet) and all respected the building's character, so it is a classic example of a 17th-century tower house. It became a hotel in 1969, and its cuisine is renowned.

Returning to the canal itself at the A899 bridge, you find the wide Port Buchan basin (base for the Buchan Canal Society) with sheltered housing and a derelict old canal cottage where the canal swings round to the north-east. The red shale bings appear ahead. Various footpaths connect with the town, off right, then there's a conspicuous school shortly before the canal is blocked at Greendykes Road.

The alternative diversion because of the M8 blockage rejoins the canal here and is described below.

Leaving the canal at Bridge 20, turn left along the road to go under the railway and then over the M8. The bridge over the motorway is quite a viewpoint: beyond the many-arched railway viaduct is Edinburgh Airport, so aircraft will probably be in evidence. The Astor Motel lies off right, then you walk through the hamlet of Burnside, wedged between Caw and Brox Burns, to reach the A89. Cross and go straight on (watch speeding traffic) to reach the A899, and turn left into Broxburn. Walk into the town and turn right at the central traffic lights (Greendykes Road) to reach the canal after about 400m. Turn right onto the towpath.

The next section is dominated by the big red shale bings. The canal is rather silted up and cluttered with litter, nor are the red bings very attractive in their raw, disturbed state. All the more surprising then to find tits working through the alder and willow planting, moorhens fussing in the canal, swans gliding by and foxgloves colonising the slopes beyond. A high percentage of the foxgloves are white, maybe due to the poverty of the soil or its chemical composition. Further along the canal are banks of scented stock. (In September the slopes of the bing chitter with the sound of explosive broom pods.) A canal is often an artery of life in an otherwise dead landscape. The brick-red colour of the bings is hardly surprising for much of this spoil has been turned into bricks, or used for land reclamation at Grangemouth, or for motorway construction. The word 'bing' has its derivation in the Gaelic 'ben' meaning a hill.

Shale oil manufacturing was a typical Victorian enterprise. James 'Paraffin' Young first came to West Lothian in search of 'cannel coal' (candle coal – used for lighting as it burnt with such a bright flame), and this led him to develope a process to extract paraffin oil and wax from the oil-bearing shales. So the oil industry began here. At its peak there were 120 works employing 13,000 people, but by 1873 the number had dropped to 30 as the oil wells of the USA began to produce their black gold. Young died in 1883, and the last works closed in 1962.

'Paraffin' Young was a chemical engineer from Glasgow. A fellow student who became a lifelong friend was David Livingstone, and much of the sponsorship for the latter's travels came from Young.

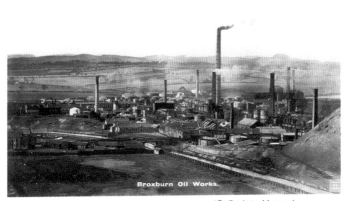

Broxburn Shale oil works, now completely gone. (© Guthrie Hutton)

Victoria had Falls named after her but there is a branch of the Lualaba named Young River. In this quiet setting (aircraft permitting), it is hard to imagine the atmosphere 150 years ago when dozens of chimneys poured smoke into the air. Grangemouth is quite modest in comparison to pictures of the old oil industry. The Almond Valley Heritage Centre in Livingston has a museum on the shale industry (as well as a mill, working farm, etc.) and is worth a visit. Take the A899 from junction 3 on the M8 and follow the signs. (Tel: 01506 414957.)

You pass a big wharf and slip with tatty Bridge 28 ahead then, just before Bridge 29, also in poor state, there are the abutments of a railway bridge which was recently dismantled. All these bridges were connected with the shale works and have been abandoned since the works closed.

A line of power poles runs overhead for a while: when these angle off there is a length of straight towpath for about 250m, and just before the bend resumes, there is a break on the right (grid reference 096737). Leave the canal here if you wish to visit

Niddry Castle (seen directly ahead on the straight). A farm track comes alongside the canal at this point. Go through and left along this to reach the minor road beside the bridge over the main Edinburgh-Glasgow railway line. Look over the bridge; the railway cutting is far deeper than the canal's!

Niddry Castle which stands near the Union Canal.

You can just keep on by the towpath, but the diversion by the castle is recommended. Refreshments and transport are available at Winchburgh; the next such chance being 10 km on at Linlithgow. The towpath goes under a hump-backed Bridge 30 and reaches the town (view to the castle off right) at Bridge 31 where a steep, narrow path angles up to the road. It then runs in a deep, wooded cutting with a footbridge over to the new, western part of the town, before Bridge 32 which has a tubular footbridge alongside it and steps up to the road (B9080) on the north side - just 100m west of the Tally Ho.

For the diversion, turn left just over the railway bridge ('footpath to Winchburgh' signpost) along the drive of Niddry Castle, a rather stark tower standing below the man-made red mountain. The castle has had impressive restoration and is inhabited. It was built by the Seton family in 1490. Lord Seton was one of those who helped Mary Queen of Scots escape from Loch Leven Castle, and she was brought to Niddry, briefly, before the battle of Langside led to her final flight and imprisonment in England. Mary was three times as long a prisoner of Elizabeth as she was a free queen in Scotland. The castle was sold in 1676 and abandoned early the next century.

Skirt the castle on the right (east) to drop down onto Niddry Castle Golf Course, and cross it to walk up to Winchburgh on a path outside the perimeter of the golf course and below the shale 'mountain' (which is being quarried, slowly, and as yet only on the far side). The path debouches at the red car park for the golf club. Don't go out along the approach drive but head over for the white (masonic) hall building where Winchburgh begins (Castle Street).

En route, you can turn right to climb the bing and it is worth wandering up this artificial hill for the view, and to see how nature is slowly greening-over the barren waste. They are beginning to be positive, rather than negative features in the landscape. I trust some will be allowed to survive, both as wildlife sanctuaries and monuments to an important industry.

22

CHAPTER FOUR

WINCHBURGH

TO

LINLITHGOW

OSLR 65, OSPF 406

Castle Street goes up through the old mining 'rows', built in the 1890s and the foremost example of a mining community in Scotland, to the Main Road. Turn left and walk along past the shops. The Star and Garter has a carved bird and the date 1903 on it. Buildings of Scotland notes 'In the middle, a pompous Police Station, 1904'. It is now a pharmacy. There's a dragon on the cast iron gulley box. As a result of the Irish influx when the canal was built there is still a strong Catholic element in Winchburgh, and the May Queen ceremony (last Sunday in May) has a distinctly continental atmosphere. The church is St Philomena's.

The Tally Ho stands at a junction, and continuing, in the Linlithgow direction for 120 yards, brings you to the Union Canal again. The Tally Ho has many photographs of Winchburgh in the days when the oil and brick works were in full swing.

A tubular footbridge has been added alongside the B9080 span (Bridge 32) and, like other Winchburgh bridges, seems to be mainly used for throwing litter into the canal. Steps, on the other (north) side of the road, lead you back down to the towpath, a green tunnel of jungly growth and shading trees (always welcome on hot sunny days).

The next three miles of canal still have good tree cover, great on hot summer days, if a bit claustrophobic. About the only features are the bridges you go under. I counted ten or eleven before there

A

23

Pupils from Winchburgh on a canal field study trip. (© British Waterways)

was the novelty of the canal bridging the road to enter Linlithgow. (A road goes under the canal at Philpstoun as well.) Steps or a scramble can lead you 'up for air' at most of the bridges.

There is a long wharf on the far side not long after rejoining the canal then, beyond Bridge 33, the second/third staging post marker. (Traffic was charged by stages, just as buses are now.) The canal bears quite a similarity to Kipling's 'great, green, greasy Limpopo River'. Bridge 34 has been rebuilt with modern concrete, but retains the number stone. A pre-Reformation parish here has all but disappeared. Priestinch, by the railway, is a hint of its existence, and you can glimpse the gables of ancient Auldcathie Church.

Craigton Bridge (35) is better than most, with some good stonework and decoration. It has had some recent repair work. Maybe we need enthusiasts to adopt canal bridges to look after their welfare? Bridge 36 is of redder sandstone, has no parapet at all and is overgrown and abandoned, as is the bigger Bridge 37. The stretch between them has clear 'kicking stones'.

Bridge 38 at Fawnspark has a car park beside it, but great care should be taken when using it, as the entrance is on a blind bend. The farm across the canal basin breeds Clydesdale horses, and if lucky you will see some of the delightful foals. This is a popular place for fishermen. The canal has pike, perch, roach and eels in plenty, also bream, tench and carp. A busy little road crosses Bridge 38, which has been strengthened with ties.

Beyond Fawnspark the canal becomes a bit like a railway cutting, being hemmed in by the last of the shale bings (bikes, with or without engines, find them a challenge). Concrete abutments on both sides point to a crossing at one time. Bridge 39 is reached as you emerge from the bings, crossed by a farm track and overhead power lines and best reached from the overflow weir just beyond. The road from Philpstoun southwards passes under the canal.

A mere hamlet now, it was a place entirely dependent on the oil industry. The name dates back to Philip d'Eu, a 12th-century Norman who was granted land here. You may notice a scent of aniseed. It comes from the feathery leaves of sweet Cicely (*Myrrhis odorata*), which grows all along the canal. So do brambles – a bonus for an autumn tramp. There's another underpass just beyond Philpstoun with great bites of semicircular masonry, now only linking fields.

After a slow transformation, the canal, from being deep in its private jungle, now runs along high, open country with fantastic views over the rolling Lowlands to the swelling Ochil Hills on the northern skyline. The tower on the hill to the north is above The Binns, home of Tam Dalyell, the lively local MP. An ancestor of the same name was a general, and a feared persecutor of the Covenanters. He was captured at the battle of Worcester, later reorganised the Russian army for the Tsar, won the battle of Rullion Green (1666) and raised the Scots Greys in 1681. They

The old doocot near the canal basin, Linlithgow.

wore a grey cloth imported from the Netherlands, which the general ordered to try to make his men less conspicuous in the field (a use of camouflage that was not in general practice for another 200 years!). His portrait shows stern features and a huge white beard. He was also notorious for never wearing boots.

Overlooking the Forth Estuary beyond The Binns is ancient Blackness Castle and the palatial Hopetoun House, all worth visits. South of Bridge 40 is Campfleurie House, a French name.

A

Kingscavil's Park Bridge, no 41, was the site of one of the change houses along the canal. The name means the 'Kings plot of land' but the house and estate once belonged to the Hamiltons. Young, newly-wed, cheery Patrick Hamilton was to be burnt at the stake as the first martyr of the Reformation. Prince Charles slept in the old house in 1745 while his army lay at Threemiletown (Scots miles, longer than English.) As you near Linlithgow, you are passing below Pilgrim Hill, and the name St Magdalene was once that of a fair and hospice on the town's outskirts. The town has spilled out eastwards in a huge, impersonal suburb, Springfield. After Bridge 42, however, you have the Palace and St Michael's Church in view.

The canal passes over the B9080 as the town is reached. Below is what looks like a distillery with its pagoda-like towers, features which have been carefully preserved in turning the one-time St Magdalene distillery into luxury modern houses. The 1960s saw much of historic interest swept away by an unimaginative local council, so this is a contrast. Liking or loathing is the reaction to the 1964 aluminium crown of thorns on top of St Michael's Kirk beside the Palace.

You come to the bowed parapet of another lane going under the canal. Immediately below is the station, then the flat roofs of the Regent complex, one of several intrusions of 20 to 30 years ago which spoilt the character of the town. Beyond the grassy area is the Low Port primary school (once the Academy) with its turrets and glimpses of the loch. The Regent complex stands on the site of the old Nobel Works built in 1701, the Explosives Factory as it became in the world wars. ICI purchased the works and then closed them down in the 1960s.

The grassy area below the castle is called the Peel, there being such a defence long before stone castles were built. Originally the canal had hoped to make use of the loch but the need to keep to its contour prevented that. The Pugin Roman Catholic church and Laetare International Youth Centre lie east of the school. At Bridge 43 you reach the large Manse Basin.

A

CHAPTER FIVE

LINLITHGOW

TOWN OF BLACK BITCHES

OSLR 65, OSPF 406, 405

*Bridge 43 is your real entry to Linlithgow and its
Manse Basin. Note how the corner of the bridge has
been deeply worn into grooves by towropes. The canal
comes to life here with a tearoom, museum and a
collection of boats. The museum is open on summer
weekend afternoons and is the creation of LUCS, the
Linlithgow Union Canal Society, an enthusiastic
body of volunteers who have done much to revitalise
this section of the canal, tidying the area, upgrading
the towpath, rescuing everything old and interesting,
running trips in the Victoria (a replica steam packet)
the St Magdalene (an all-electric vessel) and other
old boats, hiring rowing boats and so on. The
museum is a fascinating record of the canal's past and
there is a short audio-visual presentation, so do make
a point of being here at a weekend.*

From the basin you look over Strawberry Bank to a garden
with a 16th-century beehive-type doocot holding 370
boxes. It has the standard stone courses sticking out to
prevent rats climbing up, and a tiny door. Pigeons were popular in
medieval times as they provided fresh meat in winter. Only nobles
(Ross of Halkeld in this case) were allowed such, the common
people just had old salted beef. There were no root crops then for
winter feeding, so each autumn animals were slaughtered, or
driven south to English markets.

Turn east from the garden to go down a road, barred to traffic,
which leads to the High Street after passing under the railway. The
station is probably the best-preserved (and thoroughly
modernised) on the Edinburgh-Glasgow/Stirling lines. There is a
lively painting in the hall. Linlithgow had an ancient right to levy

The *Victoria* in the Manse Basin, Linlithgow.

tolls, which it had done on roads and then on the canal. The railway, however, refused to pay and despite various courts upholding the town, the House of Lords finally favoured no tolls for railways. The road comes out onto the High Street near the High Port, beside the Star and Garter (which is best viewed from across the road). Turn left to walk along the High Street.

There is a charming portrait of Linlithgow in the titular essay *Dreamthorp*, in a book written about 150 years ago. The author, Alexander Smith, is still remembered for this coined title and for a second book, *A Summer in Skye*. He was only 37 when he died, in 1867.

"The several towns and villages in which, in my time, I have pitched a tent did not please, for one obscure reason or another but when, on a summer evening about the hour of eight, I first beheld Dreamthorp, with its westward-looking windows painted by sunset, its children playing in the single straggling street, the mothers knitting at the open doors, the fathers standing about in long white blouses, chatting or smoking; the great tower of the ruined castle rising high into the rosy air, with a whole troop of swallows skimming about its rents and fissures; when I first beheld all this, I felt instinctively that my knapsack might be taken off my shoulders, that my tired feet might wander no more, that at last, on the planet, I had found a home. From that evening I have dwelt here, and the only journey I am like now to make, is the very inconsiderable one, so far at least as distance is concerned, from the house in which I live to the graveyard beside the ruined castle."

Defoe thought Linlithgow 'a pleasant, handsome, well-built town' where bleaching linen was the obvious industry. Robert Burns was less flattering, saying Linlithgow 'carries the appearance of rude, decayed, idle grandeur'. William and Dorothy Wordsworth stopped off for breakfast on the way to Edinburgh and the Borders at the end of their Highland Tour.

For centuries Linlithgow was an important leather-making centre and, like Selkirk, could be somewhat smelly. All the traditional industries have gone, though they are commemorated in the various guilds with their deacons. Linlithgow still elects a Provost and the people of the town, regardless of sex, are Black Bitches. A black bitch appears on the town's coat of arms. There are actually two coats of arms, the second portraying St Michael having a go at the dragon.

King David I built a house here in the 12th century, but like most Border or Central towns it suffered from the visits of English armies. They burnt the town in 1424. But with the Stuarts came prosperity. James I began the building of the palace and most of his successors added to it. Mary Queen of Scots was born in the palace in 1542. When James VI became James I in 1603 and flitted to London, this became a neglected second home.

Cromwell used it as barracks for nearly a decade. It hosted Bonnie Prince Charlie, but was finally gutted after being occupied by Butcher Cumberland's troops. In 1989 Linlithgow celebrated the 600th anniversary of receiving its charter from Robert II, at the time when, in England, the Black Prince's son was king and Chaucer was penning his tales. Linlithgow is twinned to Guyancourt, a town near Versailles. The population is now about 12,000, many working in Grangemouth, Edinburgh or Glasgow.

Return to the east end of the High Street. The Star and Garter is an old coaching inn, a solid, square Georgian building. Walking along from it, you find St Michael's Well which has a stone dated 1720 and the words 'St Michael is kinde to straingers'. The figure above came from the earlier Cross Well.

Across the High Street are several 16th and 17th century houses, the Hamilton Lands were restored by the National Trust for Scotland in 1958. Two have gables facing the street with steep red pantiles. Crowstep gables were designed to allow beams to be placed across a roof which was too steep for ordinary construction. The whole of the East High Street is a mixture of styles and dates with the shocking 'stoppers' to east and west, a visual vandalism hard to conceive these days. The Victoria Hall had hefty Gothic towers when built in 1889, but these have gone, as has the usefulness of the building. In recent years the hall was used as a cinema, then a bingo hall and now, its nadir surely, it is an amusement arcade.

A 1985 rally at the Linlithgow basin. (© British Waterways)

29

Just before the Cross, above the sign of The Four Marys, is a tablet commemorating a Dr Waldie, who introduced chloroform to Sir James Simpson and the medical profession. Continuing briefly along that side there are municipal/regional buildings, with a fine example of a Provost's lamp. On the wall of the Sheriff Court is a tablet commemorating the assassination of the Regent Moray in 1570. Unfortunately it manages to spell Moray incorrectly and also gives the wrong date.

This murder was one of the first-ever such deeds using a firearm and was very carefully prepared. Hamilton of Bothwellhaugh, after firing the shot, made his escape to the continent and, cashing in on the deed, became a professional hit-man. The Archbishop, whose house he had used, was hung.

The town centres round the Cross Well. Cross and gibbet have long gone, and the well has had a chequered history, being rebuilt in 1659 after damage from Cromwell's troops. In 1807 it was completely rebuilt, copying the old design, the work being done by a one-handed stonemason.

The original Town House was also destroyed by Cromwell, but rebuilt by the king's master mason John Mylne in 1668. Fire damaged it in 1847, when its Italian-style arched portico was replaced by popular wrought ironwork. The present double stairway superseded this in 1907. The well-stocked and helpful Tourist Information Centre is housed here (open all year, tel 01506 844600).

West of the Cross, Annet House, 143 High Street, a Georgian merchant's house, now houses the Linlithgow Story museum with its life-sized models, memorabilia and video shows. (Open Easter-October 10.00-16.00, 13.00-16.00 on Sun, closed Tuesdays, tel 01506 670677).

The Kirkgate leads up from the Cross to reach the Palace gateway. Panels above have the painted and gilded coats of arms of the Orders of the Garter, the Golden Fleece, St Michael (all conferred on James V) and the Thistle (which James V is thought to have founded). The porch at Abbotsford was based on this entrance - Walter Scott also cribbed bits of Melrose Abbey and Stirling Castle, apart from accumulating original old features.

Through the arch, on the right, is St Michael's Parish Church, a large cathedral-like building with a long history. Dedicated in 1242, most of it dates to a rebuilding after the 1424 fire. Its main fame is perhaps the window tracery, notably in the St Katharine's Aisle where James IV saw the ghost (a put-up by his worried wife?) who warned of impending doom if he marched an army south - to Flodden as it proved. The Reformation took its toll of the decorative statuary, Cromwell actually quartered his troopers and their horses inside the church, and it accommodated Edinburgh students during the plague winter of 1645-46. There's a mortsafe lid still lying on the Livingstone vault.

The Creation Window is dedicated to the leader of the Challenger Expedition which explored the world's oceans last century, and the huge window depicts a vast range of animals, birds and fish, including a bright red lobster! Most heart-rending is the story behind the Child Samuel window, which commemorates the little daughter of a previous minister who died when her hair caught fire as she dried it before a blazing fire in the Manse. A sister had previously died when she went through the ice while skating on the loch with her fiancé.

Linlithgow Palace's most famous tale is its capture for Robert the Bruce by a local farmer William Binnie, who regularly used to deliver hay to the garrison. One day he hid men under the hay and stopped the cart in the entrance so the portcullis and gates couldn't operate. More men rushed in, and the palace was won.

Edward I had built a peel, and the name survives in the parklands round the palace. These have seen many uses, but it is thought the water level was originally higher, leaving the palace almost on an island. Yellow water lilies have flowered in it for hundreds of years, and it is a bird sanctuary, a Site of Special Scientific Interest, and used for boating and sailing. Hundreds of swans sometimes gather in winter so the air rings with 'the bell-beat of their wings' (Yeats).

The wider Western High Street has attractive features, and once the rebuilding of the hideous 1960s 'boxes' on the north side is completed, should look more attractive. They replaced houses centuries old. This is often the story though: the Roman Wall was only seen to be valuable 50 years too late to save much of its structure, the canal was only seen as a valuable resource after the M8 and other developments had smashed sections of it.

Walk along to the restored 16th century West Port House and back if you like. The New Well still stands, though as many as ten wells once gave rise to that jingle 'Linlithgow for wells':

> 'Glasgow for bells,
> Linlithgow for wells,
> Falkirk for beans and peas,
> Peebles for clashes and lees.'

CHAPTER SIX

BEECRAIGS,
COCKLEROY
AND
CAIRNPAPPLE

OSLR 65, OSPF 406, 405

South of Linlithgow, in the Bathgate Hills as they tend to be called, lie three different but notable sites worth visiting: a country park (with red deer), a splendid wee hill and one of the finest prehistoric sites in Scotland. Wheelchair activity is somewhat limited. While they could be visited on foot, most people will drive up.

Leave over Bridge 43, Manse Road, to clear the town and take a left fork (right goes to Bathgate). Cockleroy is visible as a green whaleback. Turn sharp right at the next junction and left a little later. (There are signs for the park/restaurant.) At the Country Park Centre you can pick up a leaflet describing the park and look at the various displays. Refreshments are also available. As opening hours are complicated it might be best to telephone in advance: 01506-844516.

From the far corner of the car park there is a walkway down to the loch which is designed to allow clear observation of the red deer. They are not tame animals or pets but are farmed commercially just like cattle or sheep, or like the trout at the fish farm beside the loch where you come out. Descend to the fish farm and reach the loch car park at the western end, just across a minor road. There are field archery, orienteering, fishing, sailing and canoeing courses and facilities based on the loch with its tree-covered Dagger Island, pony trails and even a climbing wall, details of which can be had from the Park Centre.

At the view indicator on Cockleroy.

From the top of the loch car park take the 'Balvormie' footpath up through the trees (paths can be confusing) to eventually reach the Balvormie car park (tarred) beside another minor road. Cross it and pass a pond to find the 'Cockleroy' path which heads off from a wooden toilet block. You reach yet another minor road and the Cockleroy car park. From its far end the Cockleroy path is signposted - a dark tunnel so there is a sharp contrast when you suddenly come out to the breezy open hillside beyond (gate/stile). A steep five-minute ascent lands you on the summit of Cockleroy with its view indicator, trig point and 360-degree panorama which rates among the best in the Lowlands. Not bad for 278m (912 ft).

The wide saddle of the Cauldstane Slap, the rock fin of Binny Craig, the crouching lion shape of Arthur's Seat, the hunky stump of the Bass Rock all lie to the east. Working anti-clockwise, the Forth Bridges are well seen, the Lomonds are bold, behind Linlithgow are the Cleish Hills, then the long horizon of the Ochils. The big, high chimney is that of the Longannet Power Station. Grangemouth is a jungle of chimneys and cooling towers, and beyond is the Kincardine Bridge. (The dusk view when all these areas are lit up is quite spectacular.) Running away to the west are the Campsie Fells while real Highland hills can also be seen: Ben Vorlich, Ben Ledi, Ben More (Crianlarich), Ben Venue, Ben Lomond. Balancing the Bass Rock in the Forth, a clear day may reward with a view of the ragged peaks on the Isle of Arran in the Clyde Estuary. A view indicator helps you pick them all out.

Nearer, below you to the south-west, is the obvious Lochcote Reservoir. Not so obvious, but between it and craggy Bowden Hill to the north, lies a flat area which was a loch until drained last century. A 'crannog' (lake dwelling) was discovered then. Just to be different Beecraigs Loch is man-made, the work of prisoners of

Beecraigs Loch.

war during World War I. Both Cockleroy and Bowden Hill summits are the sites of prehistoric forts, though there is nothing much to see. Quite magnificent however is the excavated and preserved multi-period prehistoric henge, circles and tomb on Cainpapple Hill, due south, next to the obvious relay mast – one of the Top Ten prehistoric sites in Scotland. The knobbly nature of these hills points to the volcanic origins.

The grassy depression on Cockleroy is called Wallace's Cradle. The patriot used the hill as an observation post and safe spot in the dangerous Lowlands, where all his days were spent. He held a parliament at Torphichen, another historic site well worth a visit.

Cockleroy is not a French hybrid word but murdered Gaelic, *cochull-ruadh*, the red cowl. (On an 1898 OS map it is Cocklerue.) This waist-of-Scotland not surprisingly is a real mix of Gaelic, Norman and old British names – and some guid Scots one too like Burghmuir or Cauldhame. Beecraigs is also Gaelic in origin, from *beithe* ,(pronounced bey) meaning birch tree. Retrace the route as far as the Balvormie car park then head left outside the forest to pass (or scramble on) a rope tower before following the track down through the forest back to the Park Centre.

To reach Cairnpapple Hill by car, turn left on leaving the Centre then take two right forks in quick succession to pull up westwards. First left (a bad bend) and you're soon there. The view is even finer than from Cockleroy and the henge/cairn, 4000 years old, is fascinating. If the custodian is present you can climb down into the burial chamber of the central cairn. (That old OS map shows it buried in a forest and named Cairnenle Hill.)

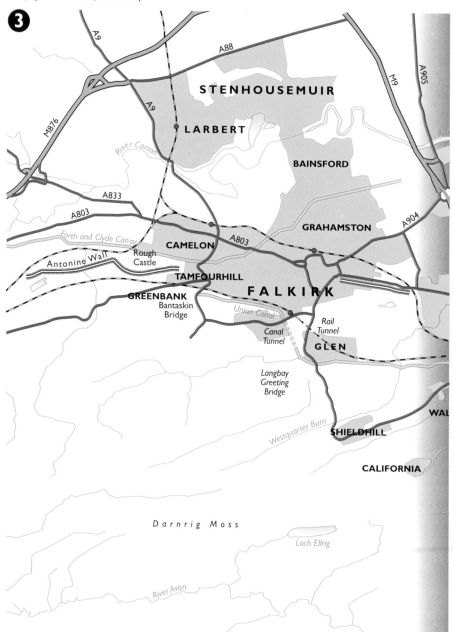

See pages 54 and 55 for next map

3

A9

A88

M9

A905

A9

M876

STENHOUSEMUIR

LARBERT

River Carron

BAINSFORD

A833

A803

Forth and Clyde Canal

GRAHAMSTON

A904

CAMELON

A803

Antonine Wall

Rough
Castle

TAMFOURHILL

FALKIRK

GREENBANK

Bantaskin
Bridge

Union Canal

Canal
Tunnel

Rail
Tunnel

GLEN

Langbay
Greeting
Bridge

WAL

Westquarter Burn

SHIELDHILL

CALIFORNIA

Darnrig Moss

Loch Ellrig

River Avon

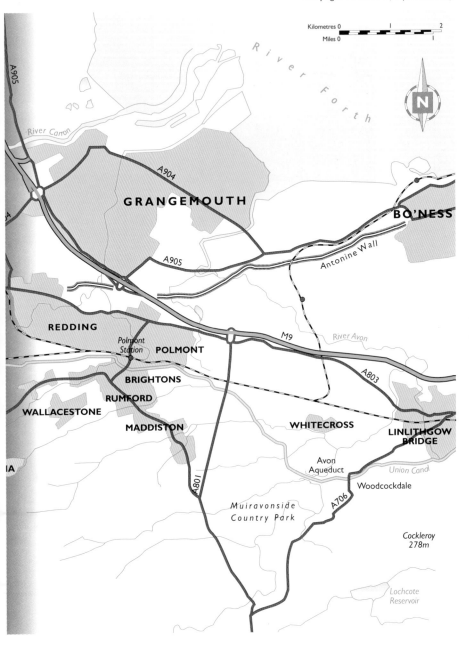

Kilometres 0   1   2
Miles 0   1

River Forth

River Carron

A905

A904

GRANGEMOUTH

BO'NESS

A905

Antonine Wall

REDDING

Polmont Station

POLMONT

M9

River Avon

BRIGHTONS

A803

RUMFORD

WALLACESTONE

MADDISTON

WHITECROSS

LINLITHGOW BRIDGE

Avon Aqueduct

Union Canal

A801

Woodcockdale

A706

Muiravonside Country Park

Cockleroy
278m

Lochcote
Reservoir

The Union Canal at Linlithgow: the palace and crown of the church can be seen in the distance.

Deer in Beecraigs Country Park.

CHAPTER SEVEN

LINLITHGOW

TO THE

AVON AQUEDUCT

....

OSLR 65, OSPF 405

....

Resume the canal walk by heading west from the Manse Basin. You soon go under Bridges 44, Friars Brae, and 45, Preston Road, with the buildings of Linlithgow Academy below. Bridge 46, the golf course road passing below, a pipeline over the canal, another underpass come in quick succession. The last, from derelict Kettlestoun Mains, leads to quarries which once supplied stone for Edinburgh's New Town. Over on the right is the many-arched Avon railway viaduct.

Some cobbling leads to the next bridge which has a wrong (and confusing) 45 carved on the east side and 47, correctly, on the west. This is a much-repaired small bridge, and is the drive to Williamcraigs (B&B). The A706 now runs close to the canal.

On the other side a concrete structure may be noticed. This is a defunct canal water intake from a stream angling down more or less parallel to the canal. When not needed, the stream ran through below the canal, as a scramble down the bank would show. Just ahead is Woodcockdale, one of the old change houses where relays of horses for towing would be changed over. The human carriers had priority over goods barges to the extent of having a rising, sharpened prow to cut through any tow ropes that got in the way. Horsemen usually went ahead to clear the way less dramatically. The building has been well preserved. There are plans to turn it into a riverside pub or something similar. Woodcockdale is a very English-sounding name, but is first noted as such in 1491.

Maintenance work on the canal at Muiravonside.

A

Bridge 48 (car park) is a much-patched one, as the A706 Lanark road gives it a hammering of heavy traffic. Under the bridge, on the south side, there is a 'stop gate', rather like a solitary lock gate. They act like temporary dams which can cut off sections of the canal to allow them to dry out for maintenance work.

There's a winding basin and ruined landing stage not far beyond Bridge 48. A swan's nest sits at its edge. All the young swans are ringed and studied. In winter they tend to gather on Linlithgow Loch – or live on the eastern seaboard anywhere between Montrose Basin and Northumberland.

The next stretch has a sad number of dead and dying elm trees, the result of the lethal Dutch elm disease which is caused by a fungus which, once into a tree, stops the water rising and eventually kills it. The spores are transferred by clinging to the hairs of a specific beetle which then lays its eggs *under* the bark of elm trees, a cycle which has so far defeated all efforts at control. (There are steps down off the towpath which lead to a riverside walk back to Linlithgow if a local circular walk appeals.)

The canal puts in a bend, and you find yourself suddenly confronted by its most spectacular engineering feature, the great Telford-inspired Avon Aqueduct. Only Telford's 1805 Pont-y-Cysyllte aqueduct in Wales is larger in the whole of Britain.

The 1823 *Companion* declares 'This noble edifice, which, for magnificence, is scarcely equalled in Europe, consists of twelve arches, is nearly 900 feet in length and 85 in height....The woody glens, the rugged heights, and the beautiful Alpine scenery around, must raise sensations of pleasure in every feeling heart'. The writer would have found the imposing 23-arched Telford railway viaduct downstream less to his delight. The coming of the railway was the death knell of the canal. Both are impressive. The railway viaduct is much more visible however. Distant views of the aqueduct are masked by the huge trees that choke the Avon banks. Upstream is the Muiravonside Country Park, a very pleasant rural outing.

The Avon's waters drain from the Bathgate hills to the River Forth. On the river below here an old priory was largely washed

Trumpeters on one of the fascinating old stones in the Muiravonside churchyard.

away by one spate, so only a gable stands on the edge of the dell. In pre-glacial times the Avon flowed through what is now Linlithgow Loch to reach the sea at Blackness.

Beyond the railway viaduct is the site of the Battle of Linlithgow Bridge, 1526, when the Earl of Lennox was killed after being captured in an abortive attempt to rescue the young James V (born in Linlithgow) from the clutches of the Earl of Angus, the head of the notorious Douglases. The Avon was much used for powering mills and last century saw several paper mills established.

The aqueduct remains spectacular and, from below, is very graceful. It was only possible thanks to Telford's ingenuity in using an iron trough to carry the water instead of the usual puddled (kneaded) clay, which was much heavier and just couldn't be carried on slender, practical arches. (Baird was able to build these arches hollow, with struts.) Once across on the north side, if you go down a little, you'll see a grated opening which allows inspection access to the interior of the viaduct. Inspectors can work across *inside* the structure.

If pioneering techniques went into these canals, some of the ships to use them were historic. Henry Bell's famous *Comet*, the world's first practical seagoing steamship, was brought through the Forth and Clyde Canal for her first overhaul at Bo'ness, where Bell had served his apprenticeship. The spectators ran from the harbour as she arrived. They assumed, from the smoke, that the ship was on fire and might blow up at any moment.

Not far beyond the aqueduct there is a milestone, 7 (to Falkirk) and 24 (to Edinburgh). Note how the pointed side faces the canal so passing barges could read both faces at a glance. The pillar next to it is rarer, being another of the four 'stage' posts, the last if heading west and inscribed as 'betwixt the third and fourth stages'. On the other side of the canal there was once a dry dock. The stern of the last remaining steel barge can be seen in the dock, but is so rusted at water level as to be beyond salvaging.

The dock worked very simply by just stopping the end next to the canal, and then releasing the water inside which drained down into the Avon valley. The modern house that can be glimpsed sits on the site of an old canal cottage. Study has shown that the swans nesting by the dry dock have been there for at least ten years. They eat floating duckweed which tends to accumulate in sheltered spots like this. The canal is very rich in pond life, as can be imagined. Immediately before the next bridge, there is another stretch with clear kicking stones.

A A couple of minutes beyond Bridge 49 (no parking) is another area of major interest. Abutments on both banks point to a railway crossing, and then (on the far side) you can look in to a large square basin, the Causewayside or Slamannan basin. Coal was transferred here to barges, the lines jutting out over the basin, so, when the doors were opened, the coal fell straight into the holds. The railway will be mentioned later. There are plans to restore something of past activity here with a charabanc ride linking canal and Bo'ness steam line, a delightful prospect. The Manuel (Emmanuel) Mine has now disappeared.

The impressive Avon Aqueduct, the biggest on the canals.

CHAPTER EIGHT

THE AVON AQUEDUCT
TO
FALKIRK

OSLR 65, OSPF 405

Not long after Bridge 50 in its deep rural setting there are signs of yet another old railway crossing. You then reach Bridge 51, culverted, so only passable by the smallest of craft. There's a picnic site on the south bank and a cross-country footpath to Muiravonside Country Park. Cross this minor road, but, instead of returning to the towpath, walk up the side road signposted for Muiravonside church: a rather stark building but with many clear and interesting gravestones of the late 18th century, the best collection you will see following the canals.

Continue up the lane between the church and its graveyard extensions to reach the Kirk Bridge (52) over the canal: a good viewpoint for Stirling Castle, the Ochils and Saline Hills (pronounced 'sal-in'), and with the familiar shapes of Stuc a' Chroin and Ben Vorlich visible. The extensive Manuel Works (refractories, terracotta products, and much else) lie beyond the graveyards and, in the middle of this sprawl, is the square tower of Almond or Haining Castle, once a seat of the Earls of Linlithgow and Callendar, but derelict for over 200 years. There's both a feeder and spillway on the canal, using the Manuel Burn; walk back briefly from the Kirk Bridge if you want an inspection.

Heading west, the A801 road, linking M8 and M9, has a picnic area beside it in case you feel deprived of fumes and the frantic motor world. Turn leftish to cross the road. The canal is again culverted and, being new, the blockage does not figure in the original numberings. Opening the canal again here will be a major undertaking. Bethankie Bridge follows; this time the canal does the bridging, and the feature is easily overlooked as there is just a short curve of parapet. The old road goes under an arch, and another arch crosses a burn which then goes under the road.

There is a clear view across to the vast array of cooling towers and so on that mark Grangemouth, but they soon drop out of sight as you walk this open stretch, the railway in a cutting beside you and new Polmont houses ahead. Despite the feeling of suburbia only a farm track crosses Bridge 53, and you hardly see Polmont thereafter as you enter a hemmed-in cutting leading to the large span of Bridge 54. An iron pedestrian bridge has been added on the west side. There is a derelict wharf, an overflow into a burn, and the usual urban litter. West Lothian had plenty of these squalid sights, but the worst come in the next few miles with the bridges vandalised, covered in graffiti and often with ugly pipes and other additions.

A modern, concrete footbridge (not numbered) is followed by a sharp bend, then you are looking down onto the railway again, with sidings and a yard, as here the lines to Stirling and Glasgow diverge, the former going by Falkirk Grahamston station, the latter by Falkirk High. Near here, in 1984, a commuter train on the Edinburgh-Glasgow run was derailed with the loss of 13 lives, after hitting a cow which had strayed onto the track.

One of the *staging posts* on the Union Canal.

Bridge 55 is in a messy area with a pipe crossing, the bridge walls a mass of graffiti, and all sorts of junk, from furniture to car parts, dumped into the water. Beyond, on the other side, is the high-wire enclosure of an HM Borstal Institution, which seems eminently suitable. Beyond the next bridge, 56, there is a road alongside an industrial estate. The canal is wider (like an elongated basin), there is a small overflow outlet, a winding basin, a swan's nest, a swing bridge and a travelling people's village. Then the scenery reverts to deep rural again.

Bridges 57 (a pipe on brick pillars fronts it) and 58 lead from nowhere to nowhere, hardly even marked by farm use, but the rural is ended by the sight of the massed jumble of Hallglen Estate, as architecturally grim as the Borstal, with its off-white uniformity and cellular structure. Bridge 59 somehow hasn't made the OS maps, not that it is much of a bridge: the number is missing from the east arch, parapet stones lie in the water and it has its share of graffiti too.

There is quite a deep, wooded dell on the right and an overflow cobbled area exits through a wall with square holes in it. A second bit of walling is the parapet of the canal passing over the Glen Burn itself. This is actually a very beautiful sweep of the canal - only the three miles of Polmont are soiled and sad - and slowly, unobtrusively, the trees close in and you are walled in deeper and deeper. Two unusually big, high bridges follow in quick succession: no 60 carries the B8028, and no 61, the Glen Bridge, is no doubt the most photographed of all the Union Canal bridges because of the faces. A long ramp from Bridge 61 is the only access to the canal hereabouts. (Demanding wheelchair access).

🄰 *

There are carved faces above both key stones of Bridge 61, that on the east being radiant and smiling, that on the west glum and

The smiling and girning faces on bridge 61.

miserable. Accounts vary as to their meaning. Did one smile at the long miles built from the capital? Did the other grimace at the work just ahead in creating what was probably the first-ever transport tunnel in Scotland? Above the faces are ovals with the Number 61 and the date 1821. Along the 100 yards leading up to the tunnel are excellent examples of kicking stones. The Glen Bridge (61) also goes over the Glen Burn which comes down off the hills to the west but, instead of feeding the canal, is channelled along beside it, under the B8028, and finally under the canal as noted.

A beautiful 'sculpture' in the canal tunnel, Falkirk.

There was really no need for a tunnel but the 18th century industrialist William Forbes, who had bought Callendar House (forfeited from the Jacobite Livingstones) objected to the proposed route, as it was too near to the palatial chateau he was making out of the old house. The building and its parklands now belong to Falkirk Council and there's a good stretch of the Antonine Wall visible in the park.

A 690-yard (631m) tunnel was quite a construction feat when you realise it was cut by navvies working with horses at best - and none of today's power tools. Three shafts were sunk so the tunnel could have several work faces operating at once. It was 18 feet (5.5m) wide (13 ft of waterway, 5 ft of towpath) and a bit more in height (6½ ft of water, 12 ft clearance, total 19ft/6m). The tunnel can be quite dark, but seldom so dark you can't carry on - but a torch is advisable. There is a sturdy handrail for safety. Where water runs down the walls or drips from the roof some beautiful formations have been created.

You come out from the tunnel to a park-like area, with tidy grass verges and well-made paths, Falkirk's vast sprawl half-glimpsed and a view to the distant Ochils. Falkirk High station is just off to

The interior of the *Govan Seagull* which is one of three Seagull Trust barges offering charitable cruises for the disabled on the two canals.

the right. There is a basin before the Bantaskine or Walker's Bridge (no 62 - which is the last), and the towpath is even tarred. A nice moment comes when the screening on the right finishes and there is a clear view of the Campsies. Ben Ledi lies to the right of their sprawl. The Seagull Trust's Govan Seagull operates from a new reception centre in Bantaskine Park, allowing disabled visitors to sail through the tunnel. The ending of the canal is described in the next chapter, after some historical notes.

CHAPTER NINE

FALKIRK

AND THE

MEETING OF CANALS

OSLR 65, OSPF 405, 393

The slopes above Bridge 62 saw the last Jacobite success in 1746. There is nothing to see on the ground, some of which is built over. The monument is a crude concrete obelisk. Lord George Murray managed to surprise Hawley, who was camped at Falkirk, and drove his forces back to Edinburgh. The Jacobites then moved to Stirling. Falkirk was no doubt glad to see them all away.

That was in a windy, sleety January battle. Culloden came three months later. The Livingstones, Earls of Linlithgow, had Jacobite leanings and were forfeited after the Fifteen but the Falkirk 'Bairns' (as the town folk are still called) refused to pay rent to the York Building Company and the estate was leased back to the Countess of Kilmarnock, the Livingstone's heiress and her husband, who came 'out' for Prince Charles, was captured and beheaded. Ironically, Hawley was dining with the countess when the Jacobites attacked his forces.

Callendar House saw most of the regular figures of note: Mary Queen of Scots, Cromwell (it was Monck's Scottish HQ) and Charles Edward Stuart, en route for Derby. One of the unenthusiastic participants in the battle was the Gaelic poet Duncan Ban MacIntyre ,who is forever linked with Ben Dorain. An earlier Livingstone was principal guardian of Mary Queen of Scots, and the nobles at Callendar House in Falkirk had to decide if she and Edward, son of Henry VIII, should be betrothed. They decided no, and Mary went off to France for safety. One of her Four Maries was Mary Livingstone.

The first bloody battle of Falkirk was back in the time of the Wars of Independence, and was the sad end to Wallace's efforts to free

Scotland from English interference. He had finally succeeded in driving out all the English garrisons, had been appointed 'Guardian of Scotland' and carried fire and sword into Northern England. Edward I was in Flanders fighting the French king, but was forced to return and invade Scotland in 1298. Wallace's smaller, less-trained force was caught at Falkirk and, despite bloody resistance, was simply massacred by the sheer weight of English numbers and the deadly longbow which weakened the 'schiltrons' of fierce spearsmen. Wallace continued the struggle, tried in vain for continental support and, on his return, was betrayed. Edward had him barbarously hung, drawn and quartered as a 'traitor' which ensured he has been revered ever since.

This central corridor of the country was much fought over, for Stirling was the lowest bridging point on the Forth and so forced communications in that direction, for good or ill. We seldom remember how greatly history is affected by geography, both in the big events and battles and in everyday social activity and trade. Falkirk as the 'epicentre of Scotland' could hardly escape. Now it is a town of 40,000 inhabitants and a busy place despite the decline of older industries. Coal mines and iron foundries made it a leader in the Industrial Revolution. The Carron Iron Works, established in 1760 (now defunct) later gave their name to 'carronade', a light gun used by many navies.

The approaching end of the canal can be judged by a white vehicle barrier across the towpath, just before a ramp in the bank where small boats can be launched and, angling off down right, a

The Union Inn, Camelon, where the two canals once joined.

dirt road, which you will take briefly. The Union Canal has kept to its contour for all its 31½ miles but here, of necessity, there were eleven locks to take it down to join the Forth & Clyde Canal at

Port Downie Basin (a drop of 110 ft/33.5m). The locks no longer exist but if you walk down the dirt track to the first opening in the trees, on the left, you can see the remains of one of them. From there cut back up onto the canal towpath and walk on again. Shortly after, the canal just stops, a rather odd sensation, after the miles of walking along its banks. This last short section (Greenbank) was an 1823 extension to allow more space for unloading goods and passengers.

From this anti-climactic spot turn down the road, which soon swings left under a tall brick railway viaduct (the lower end of the dirt road comes out just before the viaduct - the line of the linking locks). A broad, grass-lined road leads on but after a few

Port Downie, and the Union Inn, where the Union (left) and Forth & Clyde Canals met. (© East Dumbartonshire Council, Wm. Patrick Library Kirkintilloch)

minutes note Tamfourhill Road on the left as this has interesting Roman remains, described later but just as easily visited now. The Union Canal lies just beyond the Barr's factory and perhaps quite welcome is the historic Union Inn, beside Lock 16, where the canal union once took place (Port Downie). The inn is a three-storey, ashlar-fronted Georgian building which must have seen a hectic century during the joint canals' period of life. Note the mural round the fireplace in the bar.

The Forth & Clyde Canal had a longer life span than the Union - from 1790 to 1962, a complex history completely ruled by commercial activities. Work started in 1768 under John Smeaton and the canal ran to 39 miles (63km), including a four-mile (6km) city link. In the days of sail, not having to go north around Scotland was a great boon. The Industrial Revolution gave increased traffic until the new fangled railways proved cheaper, and the canal declined steadily, the last passenger services (Gypsy Queen) halting with the war.

49

The canal was officially closed in 1963. Sadly new roads were built across it and now that leisure use is increasing there are frustrating 'gaps' in the navigation. However, British Waterways are steadily bringing much of it back to life. And to us it offers a superb walkway, green and full of life, with views which will delight. Canal enthusiasts will be glad to know that Glasgow's magnificent Kelvin Aqueduct and flight of five locks at Maryhill, have been declared Ancient Monuments. They were built with monies raised from the forfeited Jacobite estates after the '45. Hopefully the whole canal will be scheduled soon, as the Union Canal already is.

The Forth & Clyde Canal, as the name implies, links those two great rivers, and with the Forth not so far away you can see the height gained already as Downie Basin is at Lock 16, and the Union's level was 11 locks higher. (Had the Union gone through Edinburgh and down to Leith there would have been a massive series of locks.) The Forth & Clyde locks are 70 ft (21m) long and the height raised is 8 ft (2.4m). Up to 5 million gallons of water flow through the canal daily.

The section of Forth & Clyde Canal down to Grangemouth is in poor state at present but, for meticulous enthusiasts, will require description. Many will prefer to simply walk on from here westwards. If you follow the locks eastwards there are 13 in all down to Bainsford, north of the town, with the first five forming a regular flight down to the A803 through Camelon. There are firm footpaths first on one side or the other then, over the busy Camelon junction, the path stays on the north bank with the odd diversion for bridging a railway line.

Lock 14 has a coping stone at the tail of the lock inscribed 'Repaired by J Wyse 181?' (last figure now illegible). The Rosebank Distillery lies across the A803. The canal is culverted but facing the road, on the left, is the unusual rounded 'prow' of the brick-built distillery warehouse, now a restaurant. The Rosebank distillery used canal water until recently and is one of the few surviving industries linked to the canal.

A Lock 11 continues the flight north of the A803. A lock-keeper's cottage lies up against the distillery wall. Lock 10 was once Tophill Depot with maintenance works, stables, offices, etc, all gone; Lock 9 is followed by the now fixed swing bridge carrying the Stirling railway line from Falkirk. The Swing Bridge East signal box for the bridge has survived, and the keeper's cottage is restored as a house.

A Lock 8 has Merers Bridge over it into the Dollar Industrial Estate and the path winds on past a school (St Mungo's), rather shut in by its wall, and then some industry. Two locks (7 & 6) are passed in this stretch which ends at the culverted Bainsford Road. Just before it on the left left are blocked-up arches which once led into the Carron Iron Company's basin. The Red Lion beside Bainsford Bridge is a pub dating back to the canal's peak period. Bainsford is thought to be a corruption of 'Brian's Ford', referring to the place where Sir Brian de Jay was killed after the battle of Falkirk in 1298. From here to the sea is a near-level plain. Cross Bainsford Road to walk along Bankside, with the industrial estate on your left.

Lock 5 (Mungalend) has a readable inscription 'Repaired by J. Wyse 1816' and this stretch is a wide pound (crying out for recreational use) along to Lock 4 (Abbotshaugh) which has been cut across the tail by culverting Abbots Road. A scrapyard, an electrical transformer station and a timber yard lead to the graffiti-covered old railway bridge from which we look down on the rump of the present canal. Lock 3 has gone. The line of the canal is still visible if you drive round by Grangemouth but is only a field emerging from the M9 and then a wide street running on to the docks. The motorway stops a pedestrian continuation from the west.

Rather like the Glasgow Branch, there is a sort of coda to the canal concerto. From Lock 3 the Carron Company added what was called 'The Carron Cut' to allow canal traffic to cross directly to the River Carron where their works stood, thus saving the last few locks into the Forth only to go up the Carron River as far again. Maybe, one day, this wee branch canal can be restored to re-establish a link between canal and River Forth, and between the Forth and the Clyde.

The last section of towpath above Falkirk gave only a glimpse of the size and character of the town. Falkirk and its surrounding towns are part of a huge sprawl of heavy industry, oil refineries, vast housing schemes and a jumble of chaotic urban development and clashing building styles. The river and town of Carron were the heart of the boom years of foundries, furnaces and factories.

It was an East Lothian entrepreneur who began this industrial revolution, but his local mine-owner would not reduce prices to make production viable. The famous Abyssinian traveller, Bruce of Kinnaird, had pits near Falkirk and he delivered the goods. So Carron, now swallowed up by Falkirk, became the heavy iron industry centre of Falkirk. Roman camps, town walls and old buildings have all gone but many 18th century buildings are now carefully preserved, there is a Town Trail for pedestrians (and a longer Town circuit for motorists), an excellent museum and the rebuilt town centre, of huge glass and concrete modernity, is well surrounded by parks and gardens.

Of interest to walkers were the annual Falkirk Trysts, the largest cattle marts in the country. The scale was enormous: 60,000 cattle and 100,000 sheep are said to have been sold in one day. The drovers' routes, from the remotest Highlands, are one of our treasured legacies. The Highlands were thickly peopled then of course, but this does show a level of population and production that could be obtained again were the powers that be genuinely interested in the Highland economy, which stutters along on a feudal system of land ownership inimical with past history and future hopes. Beasts could not be fed in winter so the great trysts saw the surplus sold off. Many were walked on to the industrial cities of England, or even to Smithfield Market in London. The tryst was held to the south-east of Falkirk and later moved to Rough Castle and finally to Stenhousemuir, whose earlier name was Sheeplees.

The Steeple, Falkirk.

There are a few sites to visit. If on the High Street, turn in through an old arch to reach the solid Old Parish Church with its octagonal tower, and the site of one of the oldest historical tombs in Scotland, that of a Graeme killed at the Battle of Falkirk in 1298. This was rebuilt in 1771, and again in 1860 when the arched crown of Gothic ironwork was added. The church dates to 1810, though the tower is earlier, and the site goes back to the start of historical time. The grounds were cleared of gravestones in 1962, except for a few historical ones, like Sir John de Graeme's. There are tombs to victims of the 1746 Battle of Falkirk too: William Edmonstone and Munro of Foulis and his doctor brother. Foulis must have been a paragon; 'His death was universally regretted. Even by those who slew him'.

The pedestrian High Street becomes very 'identikit' in character, but note the Scots' penchant for baking. Every other shop is a bakery and the town has over 30 eating places so 'beans and pease' are still easily enough found. The Steeple, dominating the High Street, houses the Tourist Information Centre which can help with accommodation, town maps, leaflets, etc (open all year, tel 01324 620244).

This is actually the third Tolbooth Steeple. The original was rebuilt in 1697, but a century later the demolition of adjoining property so undermined the foundations it had to be taken down as well. For eleven years there was no Steeple, but funds were raised to build the present 140 ft (43m) spire. The top section was rebuilt in

1927 after suffering a lightning strike. The weather cock went flying and masonry crashed everywhere, but the only fatality was a horse belonging to Mr (Irn-Bru) Barr. The Cross Well beside the Steeple dates to 1817, replacing one originally given to the town by the Livingstones of Callendar in 1681. The site of the Mercat Cross (and of the town's last public hanging in 1826) is marked out on the setts (cobbles). Tolbooth Street, behind the Steeple, makes the Guinness Book of Records as the shortest street in Britain. Wooers Street and Cow Wynd are other intriguing names.

The local museum is well worth a visit. There are fascinating displays and old photographs about the town, the Antonine Wall, the canals, Dunmore pottery and past industries. To find it, after crossing the road for the bus station, turn left and walk along to a roundabout. Across it, on the same line, is Orchard Street (narrow entrance) and the museum is half way down, on the left. It is open 10.00-17.00 Monday-Saturday (closed for lunch 12.30-13.30).

A 15-minute walk eastward from the town centre would take you to Callendar Park with its fine example of Roman wall and ditch and the 'chateau'. A slightly longer walk westwards (once you find the A803) leads out to the Forth and Clyde Canal at Camelon, passing on the right the attractive Dollar Park, named after Robert Dollar, who left it to the town. He was a Falkirk Bairn who emigrated to Canada last century and made a fortune. There are plenty of flowers and mature trees, and the large glasshouses produce nearly a quarter of a million bedding plants each year for use in the district. Beside the pavement stands the war memorial. A plaque for the first World War starts 'Over eleven hundred Falkirk Bairns died . . .' – a horrific figure.

Fun for the children in Callendar Park, Falkirk.

See pages 66 and 67 for next map

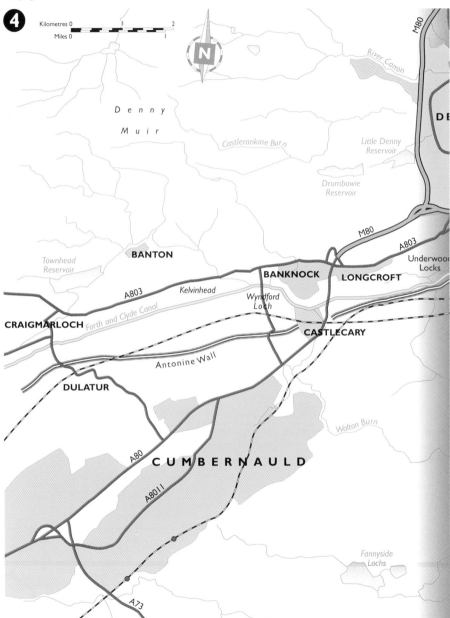

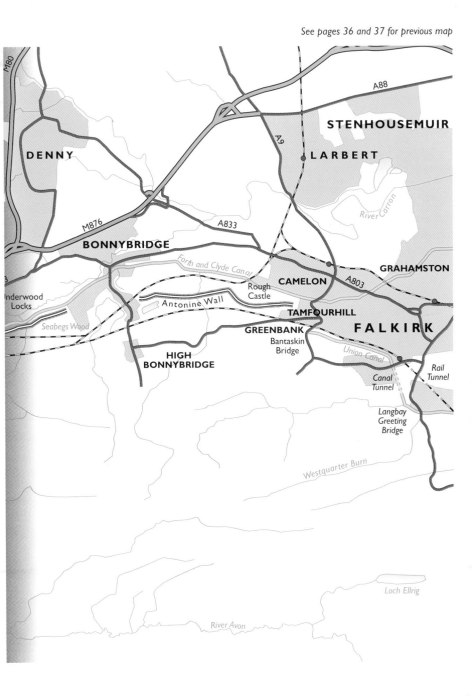

STENHOUSEMUIR

DENNY

LARBERT

River Carron

M876

A833

BONNYBRIDGE

Forth and Clyde Canal

GRAHAMSTON

CAMELON

A803

Inderwood
Locks

Rough
Castle

Antonine Wall

TAMFOURHILL

FALKIRK

Seabegs Wood

GREENBANK

Bantaskin
Bridge

Union Canal

HIGH
BONNYBRIDGE

Canal
Tunnel

Rail
Tunnel

Langbay
Greeting
Bridge

Westquarter Burn

Loch Ellrig

River Avon

Underwood lockhouse.

Buttercup meadows beside the canal, near Kilsyth.

CHAPTER TEN

FALKIRK

TO

AUCHINSTARRY

OSLR 65, OSPF 393, 405, 404

Lock 16 has a jetty and there may be seasonal boat trips operating from here - check locally (noticeboard) or at the Union Inn.

This chapter takes the canal on to Auchinstarry, the 'port' for Kilsyth. Chapter 11 gives a description of Kilsyth, then there are two chapters (12, 13) devoted to the Antonine Wall, which now runs dramatically along above the canal to the south, and offers walkers the chance of making circular walks to combine canal and Roman wall.

There are about 4 km of canal through to Bonnybridge (from where Rough Castle Roman fort can be visited): the first part simply passes through the western suburbs of Falkirk then, after the canal passes over the Glasgow-Stirling railway, there is a pleasant rural stretch, though with four successive power lines crossing overhead. Bonnybridge, as the name suggests, bridges the Bonny Burn. This rises south-east of Cumbernauld, bisects that town as the Vault Glen and passes under the canal just west of the A80 before continuing parallel to the canal (to the north) and finally joining the River Carron north-east of Bonnybridge.

The canal bends at the town and you cross a road to continue. A signpost indicates 'Castlecary Picnic site 2' and this is your next towpath destination. Considering the intense urban nature of the Denny-Larbert-Falkirk area to the north, you have won through in surprisingly rural fashion. Not far along, on the right, is a yard with a collection of traction engines and the like. After about half a mile (800m) you may see a notice on the other side of the canal that says 'Dennyloanhead 1 km' which is a bit confusing as this place lies to your right. Shortly after, down a path to the right, there is a signpost saying 'Underpass to Antonine Wall'. Seabegs

Wood is an interesting length of Roman wall, ditch and road and, if no other parts are explored, this one should be.

Return to the towpath and continue westwards. Underwood Lockhouse (Locks 17 and 18) gives a pleasant surprise - it is a pub, which also offers good Indian food. The locks have been restored. Castlecary is signed as 1½ miles (2km). The buzz of the A80 (which turns into M80) makes itself known as you approach the old Castlecary swing bridge, now fixed, with the A80 'bridge' barging across the canal beyond, the worst bit of road vandalising the canal will see. There is a largely-ignored picnic site across the road, but who on earth would want to picnic next to the noise, stink and sight of the A(M)80?

Arrowhead, *Sagittaria sagitifolia,* is a plant thriving in the canal here, and in several places back over the last few miles, yet it is not supposed to grow north of the Tyne. It will only grow in unpolluted waters, which is something to commend the canal.

The Forth & Clyde Canal was a much tougher proposition than the Union Canal. There are 40 locks for a start. The canal is 35 miles (56km) long, 28ft (8m) wide and 8ft (2.5m) deep. It took 22 years to complete. Five years were spent working along to Kirkintilloch, but the Glasgow end set problems of construction and finance. Money from the forfeited estates of the Jacobite rebels was eventually used to complete the work, and a puncheon of Forth water was ceremoniously poured into the Clyde in 1790. The earliest commercial canal in Scotland, it was a great feat for the period.

The only redeeming feature here is that the swing bridge for the largely abandoned old road is still in reasonable condition. The Forth & Clyde Canal had to have bascule or swing bridges to allow larger, sea-going vessels, with masts, to use the waterway. I rather miss the friendly arches of the Union Canal bridges.

Set off through an underpass in the A80/M80 roarer. The locals hate the road as it sliced their community in two, but it does show what a vital spot this has always been historically, and geographically: Roman road and wall, canal, railway and modern roads culminating in the M80/A80 all criss-cross at Castlecary. The auxiliary Roman fort was one of the few built of stone, and excavations yielded many coins, weapons, urns and other items, and also an altar ingratiatingly dedicated to the god Mercury by the Sixth Legion. Castle, roads and railway have largely demolished the site. The sturdy keep that gave the village its name was the seat of the Baillie family, descendants of the Baliols. The Jacobites burned the castle in 1715, but it has been restored as a private house.

An overspill on the canal near Wyndford lock.

The next minor road to cross the canal is at Wyndford Lock, no 20, and this is the top lock on the eastern end of the summit length of canal (158 ft/48m); the next lock west is at Maryhill, in Glasgow. The lock-keeper's cottage on one side and stables on the other (converted to a private house) have survived. Walking on, there's a stop lock and then a spillway. Wyndford Lock (or Craigmarloch ahead) would be good places to introduce people to the world of canals.

The next small feature is a basin cut back on the south side (why, I've not discovered) but the major - unique - feature is the greater width of the canal for the next couple of miles. This is the stretch of the notorious Dullatur Bog which the confident builders decided to cross in a straight line. The bog had to be drained as much as could be, water which now becomes the infant River Kelvin, then a huge embankment created. This was sunk 50 ft/16m into the bog before it stabilised! Then they could build the canal: the north side and towpath carefully and the water generally finding its own level on the south side, hence the greater, and variable width. A path runs up to Kelvinhead and Banton from a former jetty.

Wildlife treats the whole canal as an elongated loch, but one with a shoreline out of all proportion to the area of water. Perhaps elongated river would be more accurate, for the canal 'flows', it is not static water. The flow is controlled so that spates don't tear away riverside vegetation or droughts reduce the banks to smelly disaster. It is quite a unique environment and its wildlife features will become comfortably familiar to towpath wanderers. Top of the predation chain would appear to be man, as usual, if you can judge by the number of fishermen seen.

Pike, a voracious predator, are often seen lurking by the edge of the reeds. They will take ducklings as well as smaller fish, even other pike. Fish weighing 20 lb/9kg have been caught. Perch and roach are also long established, and tench and bream have been introduced. In the Dullatur Moss a dead trooper was reputedly found still sitting in the saddle of the horse on which he'd fled from the Battle of Kilsyth. The bog had engulfed them. Baillie, the Covenanting general, nearly came to grief in the bog too, but struggled through to Castle Cary, then owned by a cousin.

Witchcraft and superstition lingered long in this area. Even last century there were known 'witches'. A sceptical farmer met one when carting along the canal bank and gave her a piece of his mind. She held up her fingers and muttered a curse before taking to the fields. The farmer laughed and plodded on. The sedate mare however suddenly went daft and plunged, cart, farmer and all, into the canal.

A Craigmarloch Bridge was quite an important spot in the canal's lifetime. Dullatur Bog was still a morass when the canal was built, and even today the ground is wet all along the line of springs issuing from the slopes above. A mass exodus of frogs (tens of thousands of them) was a sensation during the canal's construction. The local minister was not slow to draw Biblical comparisons.

From Victorian times to the demise of canal cruises, Craigmarloch was a popular destination from Port Dundas in Glasgow. Old photographs show 'The Bungalow' (restaurant and cafe) with

The busy scene at Craigmarloch in the years of popular tourism. (© East Dumbartonshire Council, Wm. Patrick Library Kirkintilloch)

several boats, the various 'Queens', (Fairy Queen, May Queen, Gypsy Queen), in the basin. All buildings and signs of this past activity have gone, and the basin is filled with reeds. The old bascule bridge has gone and the modern one is just functional concrete.

The large building (windows boarded up) lying well north of the bridge is the former stabling block. It is built some distance from the canal to avoid boggy ground – into which the first stable block sank. A quarry behind supplied stone for the canal. Coming down from Townhead (Banton) Reservoir is a burn/aqueduct which passes the stables to enter the canal where a BW display gives information. Just west of the bridge is an overflow from the canal, the canal being higher than the River Kelvin and the large alluvial plain stretching over towards Kilsyth. This feeder aqueduct is the main water source for the Forth and Clyde Canal. (A lock spills 80,000 gallons of water every time it is used, so topping-up is essential.) The reservoir taps the Birkenburn Reservoir and Garrel Burn coming off the hills above Kilsyth. The battle symbol and date 1645 do not mark some aquatic fight. The battle predated the water catchment and during the construction work plenty of military souvenirs were found.

The most interesting hill sections of Roman wall lie above the canal from here westwards, and give fine views (of the canal amongst the rest) so deserve a walk too – with a bit more effort required than along flat towpaths! They are described in Chapter 13.

Less than 2 km brings you to Auchinstarry. Scruffy Auchinstarry Bridge (an old swing bridge) is dominated by the large, derelict quarry, the basaltic whinstone 'cliffs' surrounding a deep pond used for fishing instruction. As the cliffs are a popular climbing scene, you can envisage a lycra-bright rock ballerina being hooked from a fisherman's cast. I once received a circular advertising a lecture on 'World Rock': slides of exploits in 'Yosemite, Australia, Italy, France and Auchinstarry Quarry'. There is a basin on the south bank, just east of Auchinstarry Bridge, where summer Sunday afternoon cruises on Gypsy Princess are offered by the Forth and Clyde Canal Society. Several paths for walkers have been created. Between bridge and quarry the River Kelvin is crossed, a small stream at this level. The quarry site has plenty of parking and picnic areas.

A climber in action at Auchinstarry.

Auchinstarry was where Kilsyth coal would be loaded onto canal boats to take it to Glasgow and even to Belfast. Later, the mineral lines all converged on Twechar and then railways completely took over from the canal. Auchinstarry quarry produced the whinstone 'setts' that paved the streets of Glasgow and dates back to the 18th century. Kilsyth lies north of Auchinstarry Bridge; to the west is the wetland bird reserve of Dumbreck Marsh.

CHAPTER ELEVEN

HISTORIC KILSYTH

OSLR 64, OSPF 404

Following the B802 from Auchinstarry into Kilsyth, you see the town sign bearing the burgh's coat-of-arms, and just beyond it is an unusual watch-house in the cemetery on the left. Under this watch house lies the Kilsyth family vault, of which a gruesome story will be told later. On entering the graveyard, note the unusual lamb sculptures on stones to left and right, memorials to young girls and a change from the ubiquitous draped urn, which is even present on a cast iron 'stone'.

The road into Kilsyth dips to playing fields then pulls up again. Have a look at the monument on the right, erected to the memory of a minister who died in 1910. Apparently Mr Jeffrey 'wore the White Flower of a blameless life'. Kilsyth has a tradition of religious fervour dating back to Covenanting times, which became most notable during religious revivals in the mid-18th and 19th centuries. Few towns have as many churches. North-east from the roundabout lies the old, original Kilsyth - worth a diversion.

Kilsyth has become a vast sprawl of modern houses, but still maintains a heart of historical interest. The library on Burngreen (open during office hours) usually has historical/local displays, and the green itself has a painted lady fountain (akin to the one in Tomintoul, or Kirkintilloch's Peel Park), a bandstand, bridge railings (each different) and even house signs (one a tortoise), all made of cast iron. Just off the green is the attractive Market Square and a Main/High Street which is being brought back to life.

Kilsyth has gone through hard times, even recently, when the mining industry finally petered out. The library has a display on this more recent history. An exhibition on the local temperance movement had a cutting from the local paper in 1923 (when the town went 'dry') pointing out that the sale of methylated spirits had increased by leaps and bounds!

A commemorative memorial in Kilsyth.

East of Kilsyth is Colzium Park and its mansion, which was given to the town in 1937. There is a local museum in Colzium House (open Wednesdays 14.00–17.00, 18.00–20.00, tel 01236-735077), which includes a display on the Battle of Kilsyth. A plinth below the house commemorates the battle, but boobs in ascribing the victory to the Duke (*sic*) of Montrose. (The Grahams only gained *that* title through supporting the 1707 sell-out, and the local Livingston, Lord Kilsyth, fought its every clause.) The grounds are well-kept and full of interesting shrubs and trees, glorious in autumn colours. The old laundry has been restored and turned into the Clock Theatre, named after the clock above it which dates from 1863. Just up from the bridge, leading to the house, is a well-preserved example of an ice house. Townhead (Banton) Reservoir lies just below and to the east, and is the main 'feeder' for the Forth & Clyde Canal.

The mistaken title on the monument to the Battle of Kilsyth in Colzium Park.

In 1739, the Colzium estate factor was responsible for introducing the potato to Scotland. Robert Graham began experimenting with potatoes in his garden at Tamrawer (near Banton), and planted out crops above Kilsyth. An astute business man, he bought up farms right across Scotland and planted potatoes. As they say, the rest is history.

To revert to earlier history, Kilsyth 1645 was the last of Montrose's victories in his 'annus mirabilis'. While Montrose was in north-east Scotland, Cromwell had inflicted a crushing defeat on the King's forces at Naseby, and Montrose realised that however many Covenanting armies he defeated in the north, the result would be marginal. He had to move south. In the middle of August the two opposing forces found themselves face to face at Kilsyth.

Baillie had the larger force but was hampered by his serving a committee which included the Earls of Argyll, Elcho, Burleigh and Balcarres, who had all suffered under Montrose's Highlanders. Montrose was encamped below the Campsies, the Covenanters were on a ridge above. Quite why Montrose had allowed his opponents the higher ground is not known, but the ground between was not suitable for cavalry and Baillie was wary about a possible trap. His committee, however, felt they had caught Montrose at last and to leave him no chance of escape they began to shift their men across Montrose's front to occupy a dominant hill from which they would swoop down.

In a glen below the route, a small force of Macleans occupied some houses, and a small body from the Covenanters' column broke off to attack them, were repulsed and chased back. This was too much for Colkitto's men, who charged after them. The clansmen swept through the column and before long, the Covenanting army was in flight. Scotland belonged to Montrose, the King's Captain General. But south of the border there was no Montrose, and defeat at Philiphaugh near Selkirk was only a month away. He was to lose his wife and eldest son the same year. He was only 38 when he was executed. Five years after the Battle of Kilsyth, Cromwell marched into Scotland and, following his 'crowning mercy' of victory at the Battle of Dunbar, carried on into the west. On the way he blew up the Livingston castle at Kilsyth.

The Livingston support for the Stewarts was to have a somewhat macabre continuation. The ill-fated Bonnie Dundee, who died in his moment of victory at the Battle of Killiecrankie (1689), had married Jean Cochrane, granddaughter of the Earl of Dundonald, and his widow then married William Livingston (later Viscount Kilsyth) with whom she went into exile. On a visit to Rotterdam in 1695 the couple were making a goodnight visit to their infant,

Wrought-iron work on a Kilsyth bridge.

asleep with her nurse, when the roof fell in and all but Livingston were killed. The bodies were embalmed and brought home to Kilsyth. In 1795 the vault was accidentally opened (perhaps by medical students after anatomical material) and the bodies were found to be remarkably well preserved. They became a bit of a spectacle before the vault was closed again. I found this in a book dated 1872 and visited the site in 1989, a year when an inspection showed the bodies were still preserved.

The *Statistical Account* is very thorough on Kilsyth, and full of fascinating descriptions of work generally, and particular topics like the creation of a cut to take the River Kelvin, or the coming of the canal. Something none of the archaeological sources mention is the *natural* defensive line across this neck of Scotland. A strong wall was not needed: between Antonine Wall and mountains all was water or bog (Camelon was once a seaport) so a large-scale attack would be difficult to mount.

The minister describes the local climate as 'rather watery'. In 1733 the area was hit by a freak thunderstorm when three-inch hailstones wrought havoc and left the ground under water. The burns came down off the hills in torrents and did a great deal of damage (20-ton boulders were trundled down) but, amazingly, no human life was lost. A woman and child had a fright when a bolt of lightning came down the chimney as they sat close to the fire – and killed the unfortunate cat at their feet.

See pages 76 and 77 for next map

5

Kilometres 0   1   2
Miles 0   1

LENNOXTOWN

Glazert Water

A891

MILTON OF CAMPSIE

A807

TORRANCE

A803

River Kelvin

Antonine Wall

A803

Forth and Clyde Canal

KIRKINTILLOCH

CADDER

Glasgow Bridge

TOWNHEAD

B819

BISHOPRIGGS

A803

LENZIE

B819

B812

B812

Gadloch

B757

GLASGOW

ROBROYSTON

M80

B765

Garnkirk Burn

MUIRHEAD

STEPPS

A80

Hogganfield Loch

A752

66

See pages 54 and 55 for previous map

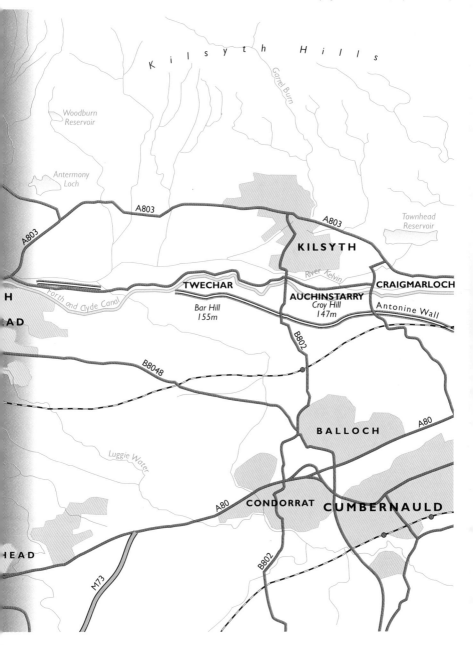

K i l s y t h   H i l l s

Garrel Burn

Woodburn
Reservoir

Antermony
Loch

A803

A803

A803

KILSYTH

Townhead
Reservoir

River Kelvin

TWECHAR

AUCHINSTARRY

CRAIGMARLOCH

Forth and Clyde Canal

Bar Hill
155m

Croy Hill
147m

Antonine Wall

B802

H

AD

B8048

BALLOCH

A80

Luggie Water

A80

CONDORRAT

CUMBERNAULD

HEAD

M73

B802

CHAPTER TWELVE

THE ROMAN WALL:

WATLING LODGE, ROUGH CASTLE AND SEABEGS WOOD

West of Camelon (Falkirk) and running on to Twechar (between Kilsyth and Kirkintilloch) are the best-preserved sections of the Antonine Wall, which often runs parallel to the canal and offers several side-trips or circular walks. For simplicity, the wall interests are described separately in Chapters 12 and 13, and then the canal westwards from Auchinstarry is described in Chapter 14.

This great Roman monument deserves to be better known. It has had a rough passage historically with roads, railways, canals, buildings, industry and agriculture all wrecking its course across 'the waist of Scotland'. Perhaps the worst damage was done in the 18th century. Before then several of the sites had extensive ruins, by the end of that century the 'convenient' stonework had been carried off to build houses, field walls, canal banks, and much else. An interest in historical remains came just 50 years too late.

The wall runs for 37 miles (60km), linking the River Forth near Bo'ness to the River Clyde at Old Kilpatrick. It generally commands the low ground facing north and had forts at regular intervals along its length. Some, like Rough Castle and Bar Hill, are still of interest. The wall was built of turf, though on a stone base, so it has not survived very well, nor has what could be called the service road which ran along behind the wall, though this Military Way, as with Dere Street, is often indicated by the pockmarkings of small quarries alongside.

The best surviving feature has been the vallum, or ditch, which ran along in front of the wall – and the best length of that feature

Opposite: The vallum of the Antonine Wall at Watling Lodge, Camelon.

will shortly be described. The main road north beyond the wall started at Camelon, just west of Falkirk, and there are traces of Roman forts and camps angling across behind the Ochils to Perth and up to the north-east of Scotland – far beyond Hadrian's Wall which tends to be regarded as the Roman's northern boundary. The boundary was seldom static in reality. Caesar had first raided England in 55 BC and the real invasion began in AD 4.

It was the governor Agricola who first entered Scotland in AD 79, with the optimistic hope of adding it to the Roman Empire. Trimontium (Newstead) on the Tweed, named for the triple-peaked Eildon Hills, became the main Borders base and, along the narrow waist of Scotland, Agricola built a line of forts, quelled Galloway and headed up to the north-east to win the great battle of Mons Graupius, the site of which remains tantalisingly unknown. His fleet reached Orkney before he was recalled to Rome. Early the next century Rome withdrew from Scotland back onto the Tyne-Solway line, and a decade later the Emperor Hadrian decided a definite defence line was needed, and commanded the building of the the wall that bears his name.

His successor a decade later decided to re-invade Scotland, which was undertaken in AD 140 by the governor Urbicus and so, a couple of years later, we had Antonine's Wall which followed the line of Agricola's forts. Indeed, several of the new forts lie on top of the early Agricola defences. The wall was held for a decade then there was another withdrawal, another brief re-establishment and, about AD 165, Antonine's Wall was finally abandoned for good. Rome's waxing and waning fortunes led to their eventual departure from British shores, but that is another story. In this section, three sites within walking distance of the canal are described.

Walk back up to Tamfourhill Road from the Union Inn. Almost at once, on the south side, there is a gate with a Historic Scotland sign for the Watling Lodge section of the Antonine Wall. This is the finest section of ditch on the wall, still showing the deep V nature of this defensive feature. With a wall overlooking the south side it was a formidable barrier. The soil dug out was always heaped up on the north side.

This beech-lined ditch is all too soon interrupted: a brick building sits across it, one of the outbuildings of Watling Lodge. Sadly, Watling Lodge appears to have been built on the main gateway/road through the Antonine Wall which led to Camelon, site of Roman forts and a Pictish town brutally levelled by Kenneth MacAlpin as he forged a single nation out of the Picts and Scots tribes. You perforce turn right, back down onto Tamfourhill Road (sign and gate) to return to the canal.

Further along, the ditch runs through woods on the right of the road, but houses sit on the wall and progress is not easy, so Rough Castle is best gained from Bonnybridge. To do this, leave the canal at the road bridge and swing down right towards Bonnybridge town centre (refreshments/shops if required) and before long, rather hidden in the back of a garage complex, you will see a passage below the canal, which actually has a cobbled road, raised footpath and stream passing under the canal. Go through and turn left along the road which passes some industrial works and climbs over a railway line – a bridge with a view – and, at the Bonnyside House drive, becomes an unsurfaced track.

Like Watling Lodge, Bonnyside House sits bang on the frontier. Turn through a gate (Historic Scotland sign) and walk over to the clear line of the vallum (ditch). For about a mile the landscape could pass as a golf course. Walk along the crest of the ditch eastwards (actually on the wall line) to a sudden drop into a hollow with the Rowan Tree Burn flowing through. The 'Rough Castle' fort lies up and right, some of its defences clear. There was a fort and larger annexe and, walking on up the ditch, you come to the north entrance causeway of the main fort.

This crosses the ditch very plainly, but before invading the fort turn off left to find a strange area of closely-packed pits. This is the lilia, dug as a booby trap against mounted raiders. With sharpened stakes set in the bottom of the pits and their presence disguised, the pits would be a very effective way of breaking a charge. Now cross the causeway into the fort. There is nothing visible except vague shapes in the turf. It was excavated in 1909 but then the foundations were covered over again to preserve them. Objects

The *lilia* (booby trap) at the Roman Fort, Rough Castle.

71

found during this excavation are in the Queen Street building of the Royal Museum of Scotland , Edinburgh, where they are, with other Roman remains, given a room to themselves and make a fascinating display.

Re-cross the Rowan Tree Burn hollow. Bearing left a bit leads to a car-turning circle and the track westwards is on the line of the Roman road. Wet hollows are old holes where material was dug out to build the road. Return to Bonnybridge again.

In the days of cattle droving, Rough Castle was for one period the site of the Falkirk Tryst, which had started near Polmont after overtaking Crieff as the main market. About 1785, possibly because the new Forth and Clyde Canal made access difficult, it finally moved to Stenhousemuir. The coming of the railways and changes in agricultural methods saw droving largely die out in the 1860s.

The site is signposted for motorists at various points. The northern approach is complex but you can drive along from Tamfourhill, passing an open-cast mine, then turn right for Bonnybridge. Nearing the canal, left, there is also a sign for Seabegs Wood which lies just over a kilometre west, but can be as easily inspected from the towpath after you have walked through Bonnybridge - there is an underpass for pedestrians (a curiosity in its own right). You may have to duck your head to get through. Seabegs Wood has been well restored, and provides a clear view of the frontier. The Military Way here is the best-preserved length, the wall and ditch are clear and the upthrown ditch material forms an obvious rampart. There is a Historic Scotland interpretive board.

Unusual canal-dwellers, Australian black swans.

CHAPTER THIRTEEN

THE ROMAN WALL:
CROY HILL AND BAR HILL

OSLR 64, OSPF 404

The Roman defensive wall not surprisingly uses the crest of these hills, and besides being an attractive backdrop to walking the canal they can be incorporated in a good walk, either done together or in the two natural sections of Croy Hill and Bar Hill.

Start at Craigmarloch Bridge and walk up the Dullatur-Cumbernauld road. About 100m before Wester Dullatur Farm turn off right, where there is a Historic Scotland sign for 'Croy Hill ¼ mile'. The track leads to a gate and then on past a big pylon. Turn left at a junction. The line of the Roman wall/ditch can be seen crossing in front of the next pylon, and you follow the track round to pick up its line, at a Historic Scotland notice. The railway will probably be heard if not seen – your last contact with this inter-city artery which passes south of Croy Hill in a deep, mile-long cutting. An alternative line, the Kelvin Valley Railway, wound along by the hills to the north, linked with the

The line of the Antonine Wall on Croy Hill.

73

Kilsyth and Bonnybridge line at Kilsyth. John Thomas's 'Forgotten Railways, Scotland' has plenty of interesting stories. Coal mining, on Croy Hill and Bar Hill, at Twechar, Shirva, St Flannan, Tintock, Cadder (all on or near your route), has vanished with almost no trace.

A path winds on, up towards a clump of trees which marks the site of a Roman fort, or you can follow the deep V of the ditch. Walk through the trees and continue. Nearing the top of Croy Hill there is no ditch, the rock being too hard even for the Roman soldiers to quarry and, later, the scarp by itself is an adequate defensive feature. On the east summit there is a big view, as you would expect, but most eye-catching is the ditch which arcs across the side of the marginally higher western top. From there, descend a spur (the line of the Roman wall) towards the north edge of Croy. On the descent to Croy the ditch is actually hewn out of solid rock (it shows clearly, looking back from Bar Hill).

Croy is a rather sad town, for its mines closed in the early 1980s and nothing has taken their place. The path descends to skirt the north end of the town, joining the B802 at Croy Tavern. Turn right along this to a T-junction, and turn right on B802 for Kilsyth. After 80m there is a sign for Bar Hill, on the left, which is the continuation – or you can walk on down to the canal at Auchinstarry.

Take this farm track (which runs up along the Roman line), ignoring left forks, on to a gate leading into a cool deciduous wood. Ignore paths leading off to the left. When an open green space is reached (the green swathe, straight on up the forest ride, is the line of the Military Way), bear right up a bank where there is a sign for Bar Hill Fort. Drop down to the obvious ditch line and follow a path along beside it, dipping and then climbing steeply.

At the top end of the wood there is a marker post and, up left, the prominent trig point of Castle Hill (155 m/508ft), the highest part of the whole defensive system and, naturally, a superb viewpoint. On a clear day both Forth and Clyde waters can be seen, and the hills to the north are spread in fine array beyond the ever-expanding sprawl of Kilsyth.

Descend the far slope of Castle Hill, passing an interpretive board describing the fort. The path then swings left a bit, passing through trees, to reach the site of the Roman fort of Bar Hill. An interpretive board explains the site: mostly the outline of the headquarters building, and a well 43ft/13m deep that proved a 'treasure' for the archaeologists. The Romans not only dropped things into it accidentally or as votive offerings (tin coins), but when they left for good all kinds of objects were thrown in, even the winding gear of the well itself, an altar, weapons, tools, ballista balls, over 20 columns, bases and capitals from the headquarters building, pottery and much else - all to be preserved till dug out this century. Bar Hill Fort is unusual in being sited back from the wall, so the Military Way passes between fort and wall/ditch.

Another notice board, down a bit to the north-west, explains the ruins of the separate bath-house and latrines. Every fort had its bath-house, laid out in roughly similar fashion. You entered a changing room, then a cold wash room before a series of ever-hotter bath rooms. The heat came from under-floor and/or inter-wall ducts, the air being heated in a furnace at the end of the building. The toilet block would usually be sited downhill slightly so waste water could be channelled down to flush it. A trip to the toilet was a sociable event - the room was fitted with the optimum number of wooden seats ranged round the walls and lined over troughs. All very hygienic and organised, and very Roman.

For the route down to Twechar, leave Bar Hill fort from the south-west corner where there is a gate onto a gravelly track which leads down to a second gate onto a farm track at a big, circular, covered water tank. Turn right and follow the curving track down to the war memorial in Twechar. Turn right, and go down to the canal.

6

Cochno Loch

Jaw Reservoir

Greenside Reservoir

Loch Humphrey

K i l p a t r i c k   H i l l s

BOWLING AND OLD KILPATRICK

DUNTOCHER

A810

Erskine Bridge

Antonine Wall

A898

B E A R S

DALMUIR

DRUMCHAPEL

ERSKINE

River Clyde

A726

C L Y D E B A N K

Forth and Clyde Canal

KNIGHTS

A8

A8

KNIGHTS

Black Cart Water

M8

A726

Glasgow Airport

White Cart Water

RENFREW

A877

A741

See pages 66 and 67 for previous map

Kilometres 0   1   2

Miles 0   1

Mugdock Reservoir

Craigmaddie Reservoir

A81

MILNGAVIE

A809

Bardowie Reservoir

A807

Antonine Wall

ARSDEN

PEL

A879

Forth and Clyde Canal

nal

Passil Loch

HGHTSWOOD

Lock 27

A81

Stockingfield Junction

BISHOPRIGGS

Maryhill Aqueduct

MARYHILL

KELVINSIDE

A814

A739

British Waterways HQ

Hamiltonhill Basin

Spiers Wharf

PORT DUNDAS

GLASGOW

Queen Street Station

CHAPTER FOURTEEN

AUCHINSTARRY, KIRKINTILLOCH AND CADDER

OSLR 64, OSPF 404

Walking on by the canal from Auchinstarry, the route A *twists and turns and then gets hemmed in on a narrow footpath squeezed between the canal and the B8032. It is still extraordinarily rural, however, the water covered in yellow lilies and alive with blue damsel flies in summer. All signs of the once extensive quarries and mines on the south bank have disappeared in the spread of trees.*

The canal bridge at Twechar (now just a village) was a swing A bridge, installed just before for the canal closed! (The abutments with seats are of a former mine bridge.) The Quarry Inn may be a welcome pause, its name pointing to another lost industry. Twechar is another mining village with no mines. The old housing scheme blocks with their square buildings and high chimneys have a certain character. Room and kitchen, outside toilet and water pump and no electricity was the older reality.

Cross the bridge to the south side and take the first road west, which leads to a housing scheme. Walk along the road parallel to the canal, passing a village store, and when the tarred road swings left keep ahead on a track which runs along the backs of houses, with many garages. At a fork bear right. Soon there is another fork with a footpath, right, obviously going onto the canal bank. Do not take this but continue down the sunken gravel lane to its end at a stream where there is a footbridge. There are also several paths, but ignore these and turn downstream to go through the tunnel under the canal. There is a date, 1771, above the arch at the north end. (You can walk the south bank through to Kirkintilloch.)

Opposite: The motto fountain in Kirkintilloch.

Shirva Farm must stand pretty well on the line of the Wall. Very little of the Wall remains visible from here westwards. Low ground or houses, roads and the canal have swallowed it up. Through much of time it was Graham's Dyke (or Grim's Dyke) rather than Antonine Wall (just as Hadrian's Wall was the Picts' Wall). Archaeology is a young science.

Once through the tunnel cut back up steps on the right, to regain the familiar north bank of the canal. Turn right (west) along the towpath, a peaceful area and much more spacious than the Union Canal. The ruin is old canal stabling of the style you'll see, restored, at Glasgow Bridge. Odd garden escapes can be spotted flowering, and there are more water lilies in the canal. The remains of St Flannan's Colliery (bings and buildings) lie on the south shore.

The presence of Kirkintilloch's suburbs is made obvious by the litter on the banks and in the canal itself. A large pipe (Loch Katrine water supplying Glasgow) crossing the waterway is covered in graffiti. A minor road (just 4ft 9in/1.5m headroom!) passes below the canal and then there's a smaller pipe crossing. Houses now lie to the right. On the south side is the bold brick St Flannan's Roman Catholic church, well worth a visit as it's only five minutes walk from Hillhead Bridge and the airy, dramatic, modern interior is really beautiful.

[A] 'Kirky' (as locals abbreviate Kirkintilloch) will seem busy after the quiet canal. A 1938 swing bridge (Hillhead Bridge) with iron tracery/finials is the town's welcome. From Hillhead Bridge continue along the canal bank. Round a bend, the Luggie Water passes underneath (as did an old railway line), a fine structure not easily seen as you need to be down below. You then go under a [A] new concrete flyover to come out at a car park dominated by the red Gothic of St Mary's Parish Church. The canal here at Townhead is culverted under the busy Cowgate, which is a pity as it stands roughly central in the 'summit' pound. Its replacement with a bridge to allow canal use is a priority need. Originally there was a wooden bascule bridge here: a bridging system that functioned like having two pivoting drawbridges forming the roadway, which could then be raised to let boats through.

By turning right down the Cowgate, you can find all the services of the town. Note the well with the motto over it: 'Ca' canny but ca' awa'. The centre is modern and has little character, but walk to the Cross at the far end to visit the Auld Kirk (1644) and Barony Chambers, interesting old buildings in themselves and holding an award-winning museum containing displays on the town's major past industries: coal mining, iron works, shipbuilding and weaving. All have gone now, though there is still a soap factory in the town.

There's also an evocative re-creation of a 'single end' in the museum. The Chambers dates to 1815 when it replaced the old tolbooth. The top floor had a school, the middle floor acted as town hall and court room and below lay the gaol. The steeple's clock was known as the 'four faced liar' as each face tended to show a different time. The museum has an interesting range of local books etc, for sale (tel 0141 755 1185).

Behind the Auld Kirk are commemorative gates leading into Peel Park, where there is a fountain and bandstand (as at Kilsyth), a good view to the Campsies, an excavated section of Wall foundation and the site of a castle 'motte'. Walk down the park to Union Street and turn left back to the Cowgate. There's another red church (St Ninian's Roman Catholic) beside Peel Park.

Colourful flowers are a canal joy: Michaelmas daisies in this case.

Kirkintilloch, like Kilsyth, has plenty of churches, sharing the same history of religious revivals in the 18th and 19th centuries. South of the canal lies Townhead; the only interest there is a couple of cafes at the far end of the shops.

Kirkintilloch developed as a result of the canal coming. Two shipyards were sited here and industries developed as they could use the canal for transport. Passengers were a minor part of the traffic. Glasgow traded with eastern Europe via the canal. Maryhill (Kelvinlock then) had the first registered Temperance Society in 1827, and Kirkintilloch was also a dry town for 47 years, between 1921 and 1968. Records still show that many of the accidents on the canal had alcohol to blame - drunk in charge of a *scow*, *swift*, *screw* or *gabbart* perhaps! Something like three million tons of goods and 200,000 passengers were being carried annually in mid-Victorian times.

From late Victorian times until World War II, cruising on the canal was popular (an alternative to sailing 'doon the watter'). The famous 'Queens' ran to the basin at Craigmarloch (Kilsyth) with its tea-room and putting green. A band and singing enlivened the evening run home to Glasgow. This is the image which lingers rather than the reality of the canals being, for 200 years, as vital to industrial transportation as are the motorways today.

Robert the Bruce gave Kirkintilloch's castle and lands to the Flemings, but they rebuilt the castle at Cumbernauld. Edward I seized the castle, but Bishop Wishart paused in his building work on Glasgow Cathedral to help dislodge the English forces. Bonnie Prince Charlie's army passed through Kirkintilloch on the way to Falkirk. A shot was fired after the troops, who had to be placated to stop them sacking the town. The library has a treasured burgh 'Court Book' (1658-94) which contains a range of historical information. In those days it was a crime in Kirky to be unemployed.

Kirkintilloch was early involved in railways as well as canals, a line being built from the mines at Monkland in 1826 (horse drawn) to take coal by the canal to Edinburgh. Lines proliferated, and in 1840 another went by Slamannan to the Union Canal at Causwayend. North of Kirkintilloch the line skirted the Campsies so you could travel by train to Aberfoyle, Balloch and Stirling – all gone now.

This book has had to use an odd compromise between metric and imperial measures, thanks to the mess that we made of metrification – but change is not new. While browsing through the *Statistical Account* on Kirkintilloch I saw that the minister quoted measures (and money) which now mean nothing to us. 'A chalder of lime, consisting of 16 bolls, each of which contains 3 firlots is bought for 6s 8d'.

Kirkintilloch had one remarkable visitor in 1785: the Italian balloonist Vicenzo Lunardi took off from central Glasgow watched by a crowd estimated at 100,000. He landed north of Kirkintilloch, which practically emptied as people streamed out to see this marvel. A mile or two from Lunardi's touch-down site is Antermony where a more remarkable traveller was born in 1691. John Bell, a doctor, went to serve the Czar Peter I in 1714. From there he went to Persia (Iran) and later right across Russia to China – a 16-month journey. After further journeys in Turkey and Persia he became a merchant in Constantinople. He returned to Antermony about 1746, and wrote a book about his adventures. An unusual *canal* visitor in 1952 was the midget submarine XE IX, which spent the night in the J & J Hay boatyard.

Probably the town's most famous son was Tom Johnston – journalist, historian, politician, Secretary of State for Scotland, creator of the Highland Hydro industry, chairman of the Scottish Council of the Forestry Commission and the Scottish Tourist Board (among other things). He was also a consummate politician and a member of Churchill's wartime cabinet. It was the war that led to his appointment as surely the best (some would say only) Secretary of State *for* Scotland and out of the war, with shortages and difficulties, the Hydro Board was created to tap the Highland water resource, a fairly assured renewable energy resource.

Kirkintilloch is another place where water is fed into the canal to keep it operational, this time coming from the Johnstone, Woodend, Lochend and Bishops Lochs, through which the northern end of the M73 passes. The canal was made waterproof by lining it with a coating of 'puddled' clay, though some aqueducts (Union Canal only) are simply iron troughs. The original lining is still effective.

Heading west from Townhead Bridge, it is difficult to envisage this area with a busy shipbuilding industry, but something like 150 boats (scows, puffers and the like) were built at the two yards, one sited where you still see a large boathouse, the other in a huge basin further back (now filled in). The present boathouse is the

The *Yarrow Seagull* at the boathouse, Kirkintilloch.

quarters for the charitable Seagull Trust boat, *Yarrow Seagull*. The books of A. I. Bowman (see bibliography) give more fascinating details – and look at the G. Hutton historical picture titles too.

A bend leads round a bluff to pass St Ninian's High School, and then you are in completely rural surroundings again. A firm tow path makes for easy walking along to Glasgow Bridge. A plaque on the wall below the bridge mentions it being opened in 1990 – the first of the culverts to be replaced with a bridge so canal navigation could be resumed. The bridge is concrete, but with attractive lines, so it can be done. The Stables was just that in olden days. Its modern status as a pub may be welcome!

The Stables (tel: 0141 777 6088) is also a good restaurant, and Glasgow Bridge is the base for two cruising restaurants: the *Lady Margaret* (tel: 01236 723523 or 01836 607755) and the *Caledonian* (tel: 0141 552 7939 or 01973 154360) – a novel way to explore the canal with friends.

The Forth and Clyde Canal Society's *Ferry Queen* is also based here for cruises or charters, and uses the canal between Kirkintilloch and Bishopbriggs. It was originally one of the Govan ferries at Kelvinhaugh, and was rescued from the scrapyard and lovingly restored. Just west of Glasgow Bridge is a basin on the

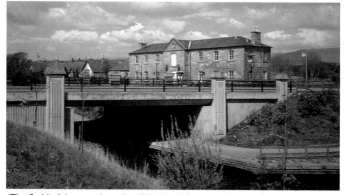

'The Stables' (restored canal stabling) and the new Glasgow Bridge.

north side where craft of this size can be launched down a slip. The Roman wall line runs parallel and close to the A803, so the canal cuts its line just east of Glasgow Bridge.

Hungryside Bridge, next along, originally opened as a drawbridge (the original Glasgow Bridge was a swing bridge), and it is worth clambering up to have a look at the landscape on the north side. The canal is surprisingly high above the flat plain of the River Kelvin. The name Bogton just below us tells you what it once was. To the north-west you look over the Balmore Haughs and the rolling lower slopes of the Campsies. Between Torrance and Kirky are some fine examples of oxbow lakes. The area north of the canal, between Kirky and Milngavie, must have the heaviest concentration of golf courses in Britain (nine at least).

There's a small parking area on the west side of the bridge but the exit is blind and dangerous. A well-made path leads on round a curve of canal to Cadder. A Roman fort site lies in the crook of the bend, the canal here cutting through the Roman wall line. Two modern railway accidents are connected with the Cadder stretch of the Edinburgh-Glasgow line. In 1973, fifty yards of track were ripped up during a high speed derailment, and ten years later passengers had to leap from the train as two coaches caught fire.

There is a car park by a landing stage as you come to tarred road and street lights. Do turn first right to visit Cadder Church, marking the old 'Kirktown' of Cadder village which lay south-east in pre-canal days. Cadder church dates back to the 12th century, a tree-hidden, graveyard-knoll of a site which is straight out of *Tam o' Shanter*. There's a doll's house of a watchers' shelter (to foil body-snatchers), an iron coffin-carrier, and dozens of tumbled headstones and monuments. The iron fountain on the gable does not provide water. The present building dates to 1830.

In the 18th century the patronage row in the Church of Scotland involved a young lawyer who was an elder at Cadder Kirk, and whose family home at Huntershill has made the name Muir of Huntershill one to remember. He suggested the idea, to us quite innocuous, that everyone should have a vote, and for his stand on such principles he was to be thrown into a life which, if written as fiction, would sound improbable.

Arrested for sedition and then released on bail, he went to France to try and plead with the Revolution leaders not to execute Louis XVI, as that would damage the cause of reform in Britain. The outbreak of war between Britain and France meant he was late back for his trial, so he was arrested and carried to Edinburgh in chains. In England he would probably soon have been free, but the grim Lord Braxfield sentenced him to 14 years transportation, which was all too often a death sentence in disguise. Muir survived the horrendous voyage out to Australia and then escaped on an American ship which, after crossing the Pacific, was wrecked on the west coast of North America. He and one other survived, though the latter soon died.

Despite hostile Red Indians, he walked out of that situation only to be arrested by the Spanish authorities in Central America. He was sent to Spain, but that ship was wrecked too. Fished out of the sea, he was taken to Cuba and then across the Atlantic to Cadiz, where the ship was engaged in a ferocious battle with an English frigate. Muir fought for the Spaniards as the lesser evil, and was severely wounded, losing the sight of one eye. Put ashore, he was eventually freed to travel to France where he lived out the rest of his short but eventful life. He was only 34 when he died.

Patronage simply meant the local laird, not the congregation, appointed the minister, an issue that divided Scotland for a century until the system was abolished. In Kirkintilloch those who objected used to *walk* over the Campsies to church in Stirling each Sunday - a round trip of 35 miles!

CHAPTER FIFTEEN

THE GLASGOW BRANCH:

INTO THE CITY

OSLR 65, OSPF 404, 403, 416

Glasgow's suburbs now sprawl out to Cadder, but you can enjoy rural walking for a while yet. There's a sturdy bridge over the canal at Cadder (once a drawbridge) with a bright row of canal workers' cottages on the far side. (It is possible here to cross and walk along the south side of the canal as far as the next bridge.) The towpath side leads off from an ivy-clad building (Cadder Mill) and is 'private' for vehicles. To the right is a woody dell, into which a stream falls, passing under the canal. The wood is a bit palsied in places with dead elms. There used to be a sand quarry.

The first canal interest is a spillway which runs into the Bishopbriggs Burn, running parallel with the canal. A farm track going off near it has a neat arched bridge over the burn. You then arrive at possibly the ugliest bridge on the canals, the Farm Bridge, or Balmuildy Road bridge. There's a big staging beside it and another set of black and white cottages. There is limited headroom, but most cruisers from Glasgow Bridge can

Restaurant and cruise barges at Glasgow Bridge.

manage to pass underneath. Over on the left is the huge modern Leisuredome which, if not tempting today for swimming, badminton, squash, aerobics or anything physical, offers a pleasant ambience for refreshments (tel: 0141 772 6391).

After this there is a long stretch with no great interest, but the good towpath gives the last really rural walking before Glasgow. There are odd traces of where dismantled railways once crossed. The slopes on the right run up to the (invisible) Wilderness Plantation, the line of the Antonine Wall, which soon swings to the north to keep to higher ground and is then swallowed in Glasgow's northern suburbs. At Bearsden, however, is a showpiece Roman bathhouse and an example of Roman road.

The tiny pond shown on some maps has been infilled, but there is a marshy area before the plethora of pylons leading to and from a transformer station off left. As the canal bends southwards, you come upon Possil Loch, which is not very visible either. Its outflow lies below another power line crossing overhead. Much of the loch is now overgrown and its the extensive reedbeds (some 'bullrushes' or reedmace catch the eye) which makes it of special wildlife interest and it is a wildlife reserve (Scottish Wildlife Trust) and Site of Special Scientific Interest.

The urban approach is regrettably but predictably indicated by a marked increase in litter, dumping and graffiti. As you near the

A unique picture of First World War soldiers with their barrack boats. (© Guthrie Hutton)

next road bridge (Lambhill Bridge) there is another 'horse barracks' (stables block), up to the right, in sad need of restoration. Two pairs of tunnel entrances that lie below it are connected with the mains water supply.

The bridge carries Balmore Road northwards and, just a couple of minutes south, are Lambhill Post Office and some shops. The continuation puts in big loops with a mixture of housing blocks, some tree-planting (and natural regeneration) and a deal of waste ground. Where the companionable line of pylons crosses to head into town you can see the remains of an old mineral line swing bridge, then you come to a brick parapet which gives a view down onto a double track railway. There's a footbridge too, and a pedestrian underpass linking Ruchill on the south with Lochburn Road on the north. The eye is led along the railway tracks to the Kilpatrick Hills.

A *

There's a last touch of the rural in Ruchill Park Golf Course across the canal. A ruined stop lock is passed before you reach the unusual feature of a canal junction, Stockingfield Junction, with the city branch heading south and the way on to the Clyde to the west. Lochburn Aqueduct at the junction is a massive structure, as you will, see for the continuation takes you down to go under it. The towpath is now on the south side – or west as you head into the city centre (Port Dundas) on this 2¾ mile (4.5km) side-canal. It is interesting that while Edinburgh never stopped arguing about just where the Union Canal should end, Glasgow traders and commercial enterprises (albeit with some argy-bargy as well) were determined to have a branch right into the city centre.

The name Port Dundas commemorates one of the major backers of the canal, Sir Lawrence Dundas, a merchant who made his money selling stores to HM Forces, had estates and interests at Grangemouth and elsewhere, and made a killing out of the resulting developments. He cut the first sod at Grangemouth in 1768. By 1773 ships could operate to Kirkintilloch, by 1775 to Stockingfield and by 1777 the Glasgow Branch was operational as far as Hamiltonhill. However funds had run out and it was 1784 before a government advance came through. In 1786 operations commenced to push the main line through to Bowling and everything was opera-tional in 1790 – a speed unlikely to be matched today.

The Port Dundas basin in the heart of Glasgow in the winter of 1850. (© British Waterways)

The heavy industry resulting from the canal is hard to imagine today. Maryhill boomed because of the canal with, to take just two examples, vast ironworks and glass manufacturing works, relying on local materials, local labour and easy exporting. One curious shipment, recorded by older residents, was peanuts for, as laddies, they took their chances: "You jumped from the dockside......up to your knees in peanuts, scooping peanuts into every available container......You lived on peanuts for weeks afterwards. The men knew but they didn't bother. The nuts went to a margarine or peanut butter factory."

The canal as a human transport facility came more slowly. The world's first practical steamer, the *Charlotte Dundas,* was introduced in 1801 and in 1828 the *Cyclops* (based on a Mississippi steamboat) was tried, but both damaged the banks. The twin-hulled *Swift* came in then, but it was 1831 before design and function succeeded with the *Rapid,* the first of a whole series of 'swifts' with names like *Velocity, Gazelle, Dart, Gleam* and *Swallow.* A cabin, with entertainment and comforts, was a big advance on carriage travel. The *Charlotte Dundas* eventually became the canal's first steam dredger and operated as such for many years.

In 1875, George Aitken began a goods and passenger service between Port Dundas and Castlecary (a one-legged fiddler entertained) but he was drowned in the canal a few years after. His son James launched the *Fairy Queen* 13 years later, and it, and its companions and successors, became immensely popular. An advertisement in 1916 offered a whole day's excursion: sail, dinner in the Bungalow at Craigmarloch, time ashore, 'dainty' afternoon tea on deck or in the saloon, all for four shillings and threepence (22 1/2p)! Dinner at Craigmarloch cost two shillings (10p). The service lasted till World War Two when the *Gypsy Queen* headed in the other direction, to Dalmuir on the Clyde, to be broken up.

The canal itself never recovered from the war, and in 1963 was officially closed. It rapidly suffered vandalism and dumping and, with fatalities, voices were raised to fill it in. Happily, at the last moment, its worth as a leisure asset became better understood and, ever since, slowly and determinedly, it is being brought back to life. We enjoy it as a pleasant walk only because of the efforts of many enthusiasts over the years, so I hope readers of this guide make contact will join the on-going

The information tablet at Stockingfield Junction, Glasgow.

work of restoration – and keep returning to enjoy all aspects of the canal. A friend who has walked many canal miles with me commented, "Right! Now I want to go on every cruiser and relax in every pub!"

To explore the Glasgow Branch as it is called, head on from Stockingfield Junction. A century ago a ferry operated here too, shown on an 1898 Ordnance Survey map I've seen, but now you have to drop down to go under the Lochburn Road aqueduct and then, left, up onto the towpath for the city. The aqueduct was built between 1784 and 1790.

The canal is high, and views over the city open up as you walk. The first interesting canal feature is an unusually good 19th century spillway: a three-arched structure, with walls on either side of the towpath, which leads overflow water off down a sloping drain. On the east side was a basin (now filled in) which served the match factory of Bryant and May (their office building survives, a listed building), just one of many timber-associated works on the canal.

Ruchill Bridge (once a bascule bridge, then culverted) has been tastefully restored. On the other side lie the pale-coloured buildings of the original Glasgow Lead and Colour Works (1874 and 1904) whose address was simply 'Ruchill Wharf, Forth & Clyde Canal'. The wharf, topped with brick, can still be seen edging the canal. Instead of going under the bridge, bear off right and cross Ruchill Street to look down on a red sandstone church, built in 1905, which has an adjacent, grey church hall designed earlier by Charles Rennie Mackintosh, an odd mix of colours and style. to the right is the centre of Maryhill.

Walking on, the buildings across the canal are of rubber works built between 1876 and 1914. They are still rubber works. (The arched alcoves in the gables are matched by similar brickwork on the street side.) When built this was all a 'greenfield site'! There's a touch of the rural as trees have established themselves on waste ground (or been planted across the canal with new access from Bisland Drive). Bisland Aqueduct, a splendid new 1879 structure, can't actually be seen as there's no access. It's quite easy just to walk past the parapet on the towpath, not realising it's there.

Shortly afterwards, there's an attractive footbridge leading over to the Murano Street Student Village, then the canal swings left to reach the bridge over Firhill Road, a stretch dominated by a row of bold tenements built between 1899 and 1903 and recently restored. Murano Street used to have factories with wharves as well, but the buildings have gone and the wharves are lost in the jungle.

90

The Firhill Bridge (Nolly Bridge as it is called on the plaque below the bridge) was rebuilt in 1990 after the familiar history of being an original bascule bridge and then a culvert. Along from the bridge, on the right, is the Firhill Stadium of Partick Thistle FC (known to their supporters as the Jags), and if you walk down to its main entrance and follow the street of brick houses opposite, you come to Queen's Cross, on the corner of which is a Charles Rennie Mackintosh church of 1899. A good attempt has been made to improve the Cross area.

Beyond the Firhill Bridge the canal swings rightwards on a long bend which was widened to form a basin and, in the crook of the curve, another large kidney-shaped basin was created. The towpath bridges across the entrances of this basin have long gone so the marooned length of towpath has become something of a linear wildlife sanctuary - quite undisturbed by Firhill Park next door, the football ground's floodlights being an eye-catching feature. A small jetty and slip allow local youngsters to try sailing and canoeing on this 'lochan'. At its end there's a wartime stop lock; several extra were installed in case bombing breached the canal. There's a sweeping view over the heart of the city.

Timber basins were used for seasoning the wood in water so, as you can imagine, were notorious for causing fatalities among children who could not resist playing at 'rafts' and would swim whenever supervision was absent. The canal drowned the careless. (It still does.) There's a story of one local who became quite a hero and was awarded medals for leaping in to rescue people - until it came out that he was getting a mate to push them into the water in the first place.

The canal sweeps round a hill on a steep embankment. The inset basin opposite was a clay quarry, source of some of the material used for lining the canals. There are several pigeon lofts along this

A runner passing Hamiltonhill basin, the British Waterways Scottish Headquarters.

section. The embankment ends at the oval basin of Hamiltonhill (the Old Basin) which was the original terminus of the Glasgow Branch (1777) and is now the site of the attractive Scottish headquarters of British Waterways, the body which manages all Britain's waterways.

There's a stop lock first then a row of old Forth and Clyde Canal Company workshops. A variety of craft are usually moored here, some being working boats for dredging weed, etc. The towpath side is surfaced with setts. A one-time slipway by the offices was the first on the canal where the company built and serviced their boats.

A A largely-restored bascule bridge (Rockvilla Bridge) gives access over to the BW site. The office has interesting literature on our canals which can be collected during normal working hours. The *Janet Telford* and *Nolly Barge* are based here. In Scotland, there are two other fascinating and commercially operating canals, the Crinan and the Caledonian, both well worth exploring too.

The next big feature is the Possil Road aqueduct (1880), but the original Whitworth aqueduct (built when the canal was extended in 1790) is easy to overlook. It comes first, just after a gate, a curved wall over which you peer down at a century of litter. The best view of this feature is from the other side of the canal, seen from some waste ground. You can also drop down to street level on the towpath side and turn left to see the massive stonework of the aqueduct; worthwhile as it is similar to both the Maryhill and Bilsland aqueducts.

A There is good car access to the canal here, turning off Possil Road (near Possil Cross, the junction with Saracen Street) onto Ellesmere Street and then first left, into Applecross Street. Possil Road joins Garscube Road (which is the Maryhill Road, A81, furter out) and gives the easiest access to and from the city centre, passing under the raised racket of the city motorway.

This last section of canal was, for a period, the hub of Glasgow's industry. The factories and warehouses have all gone and only the cobbled towpath and the many mooring rings remind us of the once busy canal life. A wall on the right incorporates the facade of an old canal cottage. Modern railings line the route. The widening of a bend points to another one-time timber basin, now rather weeded-up, then there is a wartime stop lock and the first tall warehouse, once called the Quarantine shed and now restored as offices.

The canal ends at the impressive reach of Spiers Wharf. The solid range of buildings (up to seven stories high) were fortunately B-listed, and notable restoration work has brought life back with a variety of commercial enterprises. (The back walls of the imposing row are only brick.) A century ago these were thriving sugar works, grain mills, breweries and bonded warehouses, served by the busy ships. Now the quays are packed with parked cars.

At the far end is an elegant porticoed Georgian building of 1812 which was the original Forth & Clyde Canal Company offices. The Swifts departed from here for Falkirk (and, from 1822 with the Union opening, to Edinburgh) and later it was the city base for the pleasure craft plying out to rural Craigmarloch. The canal simply ends here now, with a wide view over the city and its many towers and spires. Sauchiehall Street lies a mere third of a mile away. An oval sign gives some local information.

The original canal offices at Spiers Wharf, Glasgow.

That would appear to be all. But there is something more for, after severe culverting and infilling, the canal reappears (at right angles, due east) in the series of Port Dundas basins, beside North Canalbank Street, dominated by a distillery. These still remain, in a rather sad state, with sunken barges acting as perches for cormorants and the corners full of the plastic litter of today. It is hard to envisage the frantic industrial scene of past times. One scow has been rescued by the Forth & Clyde Canal Community Project and one bascule bridge is still usable. There are some splendid plans to redevelop the area – an optimistic note on which to end.

Even that is not the last of the story, for Port Dundas was eventually linked to the Monkland Canal, which ran out of Glasgow to the east and was built largely to make cheap Lanarkshire coal available to the city. (A branch also ran to the canal at Kirkintilloch.) The Monkland 'water' was a useful bonus for the Glasgow Branch and the descent to the Clyde and, even though the Monkland Canal has been filled in, the water supply is maintained. Some day we may be able to sit in a quayside café but, if you want to rejoin the main branch west, you can take a bus up Garscube Road/Maryhill Road and ask to be let off at Lochburn Road, which runs up to the Stockingfield junction. Before doing that, though, have a look at the Maryhill Road Aqueduct (two minutes further out), a replica of the Possil road one, then head along Lochburn Road.

93

CHAPTER SIXTEEN

DOWN TO THE CLYDE

OSLR 64, OSPF 416, 403

Returning to the Stockingfield Junction and heading west (good towpath throughout), you soon come on the most impressive section of the Forth and Clyde A *Canal: the Maryhill flight of locks (beginning the drop from the long summit), a big dock and the magnificent Kelvin Aqueduct, a conjunction of engineering skill and aesthetic pleasure.*

Lochburn Road goes under an original Whitworth-designed arch but Maryhill Road's aqueduct was rebuilt in 1881 to cope with the traffic growth of the times, a solid structure that featured in many early photographs as it gave the quaint spectacle of trams on the road and ships sailing overhead. Robert Whitworth took over the work of building the canal from John Smeaton (of Eddystone lighthouse fame) who had retired through illness in the period of stagnation. The Kelvin Aqueduct was built between 1787 and 1790, a marvel then and as impressive today.

The grand Maryhill locks from the air.
(© Dr Patricia Macdonald)

Backing onto the top lock (21) is the White House Inn (Maryhill Road) an original canal public house. Lock 21 marks the western end of the 'summit' canal water level, the eastern being Wyndford Lock (20), nearly 13 miles/21km back. There's an oval plaque giving the details. Locks 21 and 22 have been fully restored. The Maryhill Locks (21-25) drop down towards the Kelvin valley, each lock interconnected with an oval basin (which allowed boats to pass each other). On the north side, between Locks 22 and 23, is the original Kelvin Dock, the oldest building yard on the canal (1789) where canal company boats were launched, both sideways and stern first; and there was also a dry dock.

The smaller barges were called 'scows' (perhaps from the Dutch *schouw*, a flat-bottom boat) and the large barges were 'lighters'. Most notably, here the first-ever 'puffer' was built (the *Glasgow*), a type of coastal cargo vessel immortalised in the Para Handy stories of Neil Munro. The puffer evolved from the scow, which was originally towed by horses, till engines came along. Given an engine – there was the prototype puffer. The small green-painted towers are more pigeon lofts.

Another oval basin leads to the Kelvin Aqueduct. The dry statistics are that it is 400 ft/130m long and stands 70 ft/22m above the river, has four 50 ft/16m arches with arched spandrels supported by massively buttressed piers and cost £8,500 (against an estimate of £6,200). It was the largest engineering feat of its kind in Britain at the period and inspired visits by thousands of tourists and even the odes of poets. Today its solid horizontal contrasts with the high tower blocks and little boxes on the hills. The Kelvin Walkway runs below the aqueduct, but the tree-clad valley doesn't really give much view of the massive structure. (You can go down, from either side of the canal.)

The canal bends to the right after the Kelvin Aqueduct, a broad towpath which leads on to the presently culverted Govan Cottage Bridge at the foot of Cleveden Road (easy parking). Up on the south side lies a cottage built in railways' style which dates to the time when the canal was owned by railway companies. Looking ahead there is a view of gasometers.

There are signs of old mineral line crossings, and Lock 26 has current railway tunnels passing underneath just to east and west. Lock 27 is interesting. An original bascule bridge carried the Crow Road (North) over the canal here at Temple, but in 1932 the Bearsden Road was realigned and a huge steel lifting bridge installed. This has since gone and there's now a sturdy four-lane bridge, with iron girders and attractive railings. A model of the lifting bridge is to be a prized exhibit in the new Museum of Scotland in Edinburgh (Chalmers Street). A footbridge crosses the canal just west of Lock 27.

South of the lock (end of Crow Road) is a modern public house also called 'Lock 27', with plenty of outside seating. It stands on the site of the original lock-keepers' cottage. A sign indicates 7¾ miles to Bowling. Motoring, you can turn off the Bearsden Road beside the Temple Bridge onto Netherton Road to reach Lock 27, or come up Crow Road from Anniesland Cross, where buses and trains run from the city centre.

Leaving Lock 27, walk on under the massive Bearsden Road bridge for a wiggly stretch of canal, passing new houses served by a utilitarian concrete bridge (Lynch Estate) then just after playing pitches, left, discover a gem of a footbridge, an original swing bridge (Netherton). Beyond, there is a greater feeling of suburbia, with houses ranged above the railway over on the right. The Westerton footbridge comes next, a single girder bridge with a twirl down at the south end. It leads to Westerton railway station.

Round gentle Clobberhill it seems the canal begins to be clobbered. Locks 28, 29, 30 are a sadly derelict series and shortly after them the canal ends at a culverted section, the longest (excluding the Grangemouth end), created because of safety fears on the big estates that went up in the 1960s. Lock 31 and its basin can be made out, just, like an exposed archaeological site. (Clobberhill, Garscadden and Boghouse Locks are scheduled for renewal so this area may well have improved by the time you read this or walk the section.)

Cross Blairdardie Road (nearby shop) and follow the attractive roll of 'park' past a sports centre and school to reach the A82 Great Western Road, milestoned with four large tower blocks. There's a play area as this busy road is reached. It is a dual carriageway and great care should be taken in crossing; best to use the nearby pedestrian crossing lights.

Regain the canal and walk along a pleasant section with impressive new flats by the far bank, with the tower blocks behind. There's a trim bascule bridge at Bard Avenue; the word bascule comes from the French for a see-saw. This design was used to satisfy the needs of cattle droving. The cows wouldn't cross some other types of bridge. At the end of the new flats you come

West from Duntreath Road in Glasgow.

on the last flight of locks (Boghouse: nos 33-35) which have a surviving lock-keepers' cottage. There's a wee shop then a sports field on the left.

Lock 36 (Boghouse) is left high and dry as the canal is once more
culverted, under Duntreath Road. The Great Western Road is just
off to the right. Pedestrians are culverted as well, with a touch of
graffiti, to come out on a well-manicured reach, with a path on
both sides. The canal is reduced to one metre in depth. Out on the
right, beyond playing fields, is the shopping area of Old
Drumchapel. As Glasgow Airport lies just across the Clyde, there
are usually aircraft in evidence.

Another bascule bridge is passed (Linnvale), the 'park' now a
narrow strip, still pathed on both banks, heavily defended from a
school (north) and the large Thor works (south), then there's a
sprawl of superstores and the like on the north flank and more
works off left. Ahead, the eye is caught by a church which looks
like a fire station, and this marks one of the more extraordinary
stretches of canal walking. Cross a busy road (Whitecrook Street),
where the Glasgow-Loch Lomond cycleway joins the route (its
signs will be seen hereafter) but this time there are pedestrian
crossing lights.

Immediately beyond, you are in the vast Clyde Shopping
Centre. On the north bank is 'moored' the *Debra Rose*
(McMonagles Fish & Chips, open 11.00-17.00) and there are
plenty of big stores and shops, to the extent that the canal is
crossed by a shopping mall! A familiar oval indicates 3¾ miles to
Bowling. Looking left along the Sylvania Way (the vaulted mall)
a crane is almost a symbol to have in view, for you are now in
Clydebank where many great ships such as the *Lusitania*, the
Queen Mary and the *QE2* were built. The area was devastated by
wartime bombing (4,000 houses destroyed) and has suffered
from the steady decline in shipbuilding. The canal is almost a
reflecting pool in this surprising setting and what buzz of life
could come to Port Dundas if something similar could be
created.

The canal is culverted for the busy Kilbowie Road, but there are
pedestrian lights at the crossing. Beyond, the canal is well
'rehabitated' in planners' parlance, as if the canals had been
naughty and had to be made acceptable again. Looking back over
the grassy area (left) the tower of the Clydebank Municipal
Buildings can be seen. The storms of 1968 saw the angel on top,
which came from the 1901 Glasgow exhibition, removed. The
north side of the canal has a high concrete wall running along to
an abutment of an old bridge. A railway runs alongside on the left,
with a branch bearing off into the docks, and this soon passes
below the canal, the tunnel only noted from the towpath as there's
a brick wall. The view along the line leads the eye back to the
cranes of Clydebank.

A Shortly after, the canal crosses a minor road. Steps descend onto Boquharan Road. It is worth going down to see two things: the unusual narrow, brick bridge with its raised pedestrian way and, across the Dumbarton Road, on the wall above the Park Tavern, an interesting carved feature showing a First World War battleship.

A You pass some good modern iron railings, then a footbridge (Trafalgar Street), with the big flats of Dalmuir looming ahead. The canal swings sharp left to the culverted Dumbarton Road. There used to be a swing bridge here, with tram lines, and it was odd that trams and canals both ceased to operate at the same time. Originally there was just a bascule bridge.

Cross at the pedestrian lights to regain the towpath beside the Clydebank Industrial Estate on Beardmore Street. The long straight that follows gives a view to the Erskine Bridge, the Kilpatrick Hills draw closer, and there's a quieter feel to the finishing miles. Ironically, this last section (almost as level as the Union Canal) was soon largely unnecessary once the Clyde was regularly dredged to allow sea-going ships up into the city. Had dredging come earlier, the Forth and Clyde canal might have ended in the city below Port Dundas.

Just before a pretty bascule bridge (Dalmuir West), a curve of decayed wall points to the Duntocher Burn passing under the canal. Power lines pass overhead. On the left there is some dereliction with first glimpses of the river, an area which is being turned into a wildlife centre, the Saltings. At a spot where there are two benches by the towpath, you can go over a bridge across a derelict railway track to get a good view of the Erskine Bridge.

A Before this high-striding bridge was built, there was a vehicle ferry across the Clyde. Vehicles then crossed the canal by the Dalnottar Bridge, a sturdy 1934 swing bridge, still in good shape, with an attractive white cottage beside it. If you turn left it is only two minutes walk to reach the ferry site and the most impressive close view of the Erskine Bridge. Opened in 1971, it has somehow never caught the popular imagination like the Forth Bridge, but is still big and bold, as one guide puts it: "elegant in the distant landscape but awesomely monstrous above the village". In the 19th century a ferryboat could carry up to 40 head of cattle and was pulled across on a chain.

Almost under the stilt-walking bridge is the fully restored Old Kilpatrick Lock (37, only two to come), with a BW interpretive board. Five minutes walk further on is a strong raised wooden Saltings walkway off to the left which allows you a view of the Erskine Bridge from a new angle. Old Kilpatrick nestles below the hills with the clock tower of the church a prominent landmark. Saint Patrick was supposedly born here. Next comes the penultimate Ferrydyke bascule bridge. One of the bridge-keepers' cottages has survived, but the one-time stables are ruinous. The bank on the north side was the site of the terminal fort of the Antonine Wall which, running along at about big bridge level, descended to the Clyde here. Strange how these two great engineering feats, separated by so many centuries, have marched together across Scotland.

On a winter walk this way I once watched two young swans fly in to land on the canal; they presumed it was water and it was only when they put down their big feet they discovered the canal was frozen solid. The sight of swans sliding along on their bottoms, on their necks, and round and round, reduced spectators to hysterics.

The attractive Kilpatrick Hills are close to the canal now and a railing shows where a burn, coming off the slopes, passes under the canal. Suddenly you come on the final features: a landing-stage (and boats as like as not) beside a car park and a large white house, with red sandstone quoins. Lock 38 leads into a big, high-walled basin with the last bascule bridge at its end, then the arches of an abandoned railway (a swing bridge when operational) lead to the boat-crowded last basin itself. This can be marina-busy and, in winter, many boats are moored there for the season with the yachties busy working on them at weekends. It's a very attractive scene (there's an extraordinary mix of craft) though one writer calls it a "tired jauntiness".

Circumambulating the basin you come onto an overflow, which was once the original sea lock (39). Between two and five million gallons of water flows through the Forth and Clyde canal system each day. The view up-river is always fine, with the Erskine Bridge seen at its very best. Cross the present Lock 39 (or should it be 40?) which leads out to Bowling Harbour. On the point down-river is a monument to Henry Bell, of the *Comet* steamship fame. (The *Comet* was wrecked on Craignish Point in 1820 while operating a Glasgow-Fort William service through the Crinan Canal.) The trim 18th century Customs House is passed before yo go under the abandoned railway again to arrive back at the bascule bridge. The arches contain workshops, stores, a chandler's and a seasonal café.

Your canal walk is over. To celebrate the opening of the full canal in 1790, a hogshead of Forth water was poured into the Clyde. Your celebrations will no doubt be more modest.

To leave, take the track from the bascule bridge left (not the track tight against the railway arches - that's the vehicle access to the harbour basin) to climb up and over the busy railway line. The Glenarbuck Burn comes racing off the Kilpatrick Hills beside you as you reach the Bowling road (A814). There's a small snack bar and, across the road, a bus stop for buses back to Clydebank/ Glasgow, a service operating about every quarter of an hour.

There is rather limited car parking by the canal basins and care should be taken not to block access. It is easy to miss the turn-off from the A814, but if you overshoot, the village of Bowling follows where you can turn and try again, or perhaps park there for convenience.

The old Customs House at the Bowling Basin.

PRACTICAL INFORMATION

TOURIST INFORMATION

Edinburgh: Tourist Information Centre, 3 Princes Street, Edinburgh EH2 2QP. Tel: 0131 557 2727.
Linlithgow: Burgh Halls, The Cross, High Street, Linlithgow EH49 7EJ. Tel: 01506 844600.
Falkirk: The Steeple, 2-4 Glebe Street, Falkirk FK1 1NN. Tel: 01324 620244.
Glasgow: 35 St Vincent Place, Glasgow G1 2ER. Tel: 0141 204 4400.

ACCOMMODATION

The Tourist Information Centres are happy to supply up-to-date brochures on accommodation. With bus and/or train routes often running in parallel with the canals, you should be able to return to either Edinburgh or Glasgow if desired. Both cities have SYHA and private hostels offering cheaper accommodation. It also pays to ask locally: not all B&Bs will be on the official lists.

BODIES USING OR SUPPORTING THE CANALS

British Waterways, Canal House, The Old Basin, 1 Applecross Street, Glasgow G4 9SP. Tel: 0141 332 6936. Owners and licensees for use of the water, ranger service, will arrange talks, events, etc. Broxburn Office: Station Road, Broxburn, West Lothian EH52 5PG. Tel: 01506-857725.
Buchan Canal Society, 22 Union Road, Broxburn EH52 6HR.
Edinburgh Canal Centre, Ratho (Bridge Inn). Tel: 0131 333 1320/1251.
Forth Canoe Club, 3 Westhall Gardens, Edinburgh EH10 4JJ. Tel: 0131 228 5138.
Forth and Clyde Canal Society, 8 Kelvin Way, Kirkintilloch, Glasgow G66 1DX. Tel: 0141 776 3812.
Forth and Clyde Canoe Club, Community Central Hall, 304 Maryhill Road, Glasgow G20 7YE. Tel: 0141 332 9115 (ext 19).
Forth and Clyde Canal Community Project: as for F & C CC.
Linlithgow Union Canal Society (LUCS), Manse Road Basin, Linlithgow, West Lothian EH49 6AJ. Tel: 01506 671215.
Restaurant cruises: see text under Ratho and Glasgow Bridge.

Scottish Inland Waterways Association, 139 Old Dalkeith Road, Edinburgh EH16 4SZ. Tel: 0131 664 1070.
Seagull Trust, Princes House, 5 Shandwick Place, Edinburgh EH2 4RG. Tel: 0131 229 1789.

OTHER USEFUL CONTACTS
Scotrail, Glasgow: 0141 204 2844.
Scotrail, Edinburgh: 0345 484950.
Tramline, Edinburgh: 0131 225 3858.
Linlithgow bus station: 01506 842167.
Falkirk bus station: 01324 623985.
Edinburgh bus station, St Andrews Square: 0131 558 1616.
Glasgow bus station, Buchanan Street: 0141 332 7133.

BIBLIOGRAPHY
Local libraries always order books for readers if requested. This is a selected list, but each book itself will lead on to others. The Tourist Information Centres on or near the route are a useful source of new local booklets.

Anderson, R.: A History of Kilsyth. Duncan,1901.
Anton, P.: *Kilsyth, A Parish History.* John Smith,1843 (reprinted).
Bowman, A.I.: *Kirkintilloch Shipbuilding.* Strathkelvin District Publications,1983.
Bowman, A.I.: *Swifts and Queens: Passenger Transport on the Forth & Clyde Canal.* Strathkelvin Dist Pubs,1984.
Bowman, A.I.: *The Gipsy o' Kirky.* Strathkelvin Dist Pubs, 1987.
Buildings of Scotland series (Penguin) has comprehensive coverage of *Edinburgh, Lothian and Glasgow.*
Carter, P. (editor): *Forth & Clyde Canal Guidebook.* Forth & Clyde Canal Society, 1991.
Companion for Canal Passengers Betwixt Edinburgh and Glasgow, 1823. Facsimile, LUCS booklet, 1981.
Haldane, A.R.B.: *The Drove Roads of Scotland.* David & Charles, 1973 et seq. (a classic).
Hanson, W.H. and Maxwell, G.S.: *Rome's North-West Frontier - The Antonine Wall.* EUP,1983.
Hendrie, W.F.: *Discovering West Lothian.* John Donald,1986.
Hendrie, W.F.: *Linlithgow, Six Hundred Years a Royal Burgh.* John Donald, 1989.
Hume, J.R.: *The Industrial Archaeology of Scotland. 1: The Lowlands and Borders.* Batsford,1976.
Hutchison, J.: *Weavers, Miners and the Open Book.* Cumbernauld, 1986 (Kilsyth history).
Hutton, G.: *The Union Canal* (Stenlake); *A Forth & Clyde Canalbum* (Stenlake) (old pictures).
Johnstone, Anne: *The Wild Frontier.* Mowbray House, 1986. (Large format, illustrated, introduction to the Roman Wall.)

Lawson, L.: *A History of Falkirk*. Falkirk,1975.

Love, D.: *Scottish Kirkyards*. Hale,1989.

Martin, D.: *The Story of Kirkintilloch*. Strathkelvin Dist. Pubs, 1980.

Martin, D.: *The Forth and Clyde Canal: A Kirkintilloch View*. Strathkelvin Dist. Pubs, 1985.

Massey, A.: *The Edinburgh & Glasgow Union Canal*. Falkirk Museum, 1983.

Robertson, A.J.: *The Antonine Wall*. Glasgow Archaeological Soc, 1990 (useful field guide).

Skinner, B.C.: *The Union Canal, A Report*. LUCS, 1977.

Smith, R.: *25 Walks, Edinburgh and Lothian*. HMSO,1995.

(Old) Statistical Account of Scotland: Edited by John Sinclair 1791-99 and reprinted in 1980s by E.P. Publishing by areas; Volume 2 covers the *Lothians*; Vol 9 covers *Dunbartonshire, Stirlingshire and Clackmannanshire*.

Thomas, D. St J.: *Forgotten Railways, Scotland*. David & Charles.

Tranter, N.: *Portrait of the Lothians*. Hale, 1979.

Waldie, G.: *A History of the Town and Palace of Linlithgow*, 1897 /1982.

Watson, T.: *Kirkintilloch: Town and Parish*. John Smith, Glasgow, 1894.

Williamson, A.G.: *Twixt Forth and Clyde*. London, 1944.

Willsher, B.: *Understanding Scottish Graveyards*. Chambers, 1985.

CANAL COUNTRY CODE

Good manners and friendliness are the basics to ensure safety on canal towpaths. Think of other users. The Country Code is a charter of freedom, not a restriction.

Canal byelaws do not allow horse-riding, motorbike or vehicle use of the towpath. This is obviously in the interests of safety as well as enjoyment. Cycles have no right of way and should display a (free) BW permit for the stretches allowed. Cyclists should take care not to startle walkers (coming from behind or round blind corners) and treat bridges and locks with great care, as indeed should pedestrians, who should also let fishermen know of their approach. Anglers should be careful not to interfere with other users. Beware of overhead power-lines.

Close all gates. There is nothing calculated to annoy farmers more than having to round up strayed livestock. Don't go over walls, or through fences or hedges – there are few places without gates or stiles on our route.

Leave livestock, crops, boats and machinery alone.

Guard against all risk of fires.

Dump your litter in bins, not in the countryside or the canal. You'll see some bad sights – don't add to them. Poly bags can mean death to a grazing cow, broken glass is wicked for both man and beast, and drink cans an insufferable eyesore.

Leave wildlife alone. Collect memories, not specimens.

Walk quietly in the countryside. Nature goes unobtrusively and you'll see far more if you are not clad in garish colours and walking with a ghetto blaster. (I joke not – I've met plenty on the towpaths.)

Dogs need strict control and should not be allowed to foul the towpath.

Be extra careful when walking on roads, however quiet these appear. Manic drivers are no respecters of pedestrians.

Make local contacts. Rural people are still sociable and a 'crack' will often be welcomed. Use the Tourist Information Centres and bookshops along the way to widen knowledge and enrich your experience. Local people met in bars and cafés are often a fund of information.

THE FUTURE...

The Millenium Fund is making a large grant towards the full restoration of the two canals so major, exciting developments will see out the 1990's. Celebrate, participate.

The Leamington lifting bridge, Edinburgh.

INDEX

Printed in Scotland for The Stationery Office by CC. No. 70343 50C 4/97